HUMAN RESOURCES DISPUTES & RESOLUTIONS

HUMAN RESOURCES
DISPUTES &
RESOLUTIONS

THE MANAGER'S GUIDE TO
EMPLOYMENT HEADACHES & THE LAW

HARRY SHERRARD

KOGAN PAGE

First published in Great Britain in 2007 by Kogan Page Limited

120 Pentonville Road
London N1 9JN
United Kingdom
www.kogan-page.co.uk

© Harry Sherrard, 2007

British Library Cataloguing in Publication Data

A CIP record for this book is available from the British Library.

ISBN-10   0 7494 4963 2
ISBN-13   978 0 7494 4963 6

Typeset by JS Typesetting Ltd, Porthcawl, Mid Glamorgan
Printed and bound in India by Replika Press Pvt Ltd

Contents

Preface

I founded my law firm, Sherrards, in 1999, on the back of several years as partner and head of employment law at a regional practice. My vision for the firm was one that bridged the gap between the legal side and human resources practice; hence the firm's strapline was 'Employment Law and Human Resources'. As well as lawyers, I established working relationships with a team of very competent HR consultants, and we worked jointly on a number of projects – training events, redundancy and restructuring programmes, recruitment exercises and general troubleshooting.

In promoting Sherrards and the range of services we offered, I identified the need to offer public training events that gave more to delegates than the standard fare served up by law firms. Legal updates are important, but increasingly available through means other than attending seminars; the development of online resources in particular. What I felt was of greater value to HR practitioners and line managers with people responsibilities was to share with them my experience of tackling workplace disputes, problems and dilemmas, and to demonstrate to them our practical strategies for resolution. To achieve this I saw the need to create a training course that was both written and delivered in a completely new style. And so 'Employment Headaches' was born.

Seema Barker, the first solicitor employee of Sherrards, and I wrote and presented our first 'Employment Headaches' course in 2001, with immediate success. Audiences loved our case-study-driven, participative approach. Rather than the traditional lawyer monologue, delegates received during the course only the questions; and were challenged to come up with their own suggestions as to how the situations should be resolved. Seema and I would then work through the different proposals from the audience, making sure that the outcomes were legally compliant as well as practical, and achieving the best result for the employer. Time and again we were told by delegates that their learning at our

Employment Headaches event was far greater, and of much more relevant application, than other employment law presentations that they had attended.

It is fair to say that the events were fun for Seema and me as well; we enjoyed creating our Headaches, and running the events. Seema's 'cute little skirts' Headache on page 13 remains one of my favourites. And it is a classic Headache in every sense; not one to which there is a prescriptive, right or wrong answer, but where judgement and experience are brought to bear. Often it provokes lively discussion and contradictory viewpoints! But that is the beauty of the Headaches approach. Delegates can hear and benefit from the knowledge and expertise not only of the lawyers, but also the other delegates, who are often senior HR professionals with a wealth of experience.

As Sherrards grew and more lawyers joined us, they were all schooled in the Employment Headaches approach, and our events enjoyed continued success. Every autumn saw us writing a new course, and by 2006 I realized that we had written enough Headaches to turn our questions and answers into a book, thereby bringing the learning to a much wider audience.

Human Resources Disputes and Resolutions is a compilation of the best Headaches we used in our courses over the past five years, all updated, and some substantially rewritten to reflect developments in the law. They also benefit from input arising out of the running of the courses themselves; as I have explained, often a senior HR professional at our events makes an interesting comment, which we later incorporate into the answers.

The book successfully captures the essence of the courses, through a series of thought-provoking case studies, and answers that are a combination of legal analysis and, more importantly, the practical application of that legal analysis to the situation encountered.

In this, I think *Human Resources Disputes and Resolutions* is a unique learning opportunity, for both developing HR professionals and line managers with people responsibilities. Indeed, we have worked hard to make the book all things to all people. Absolute beginners in employment law will be guided through the essence of, for example, how to handle a straightforward unfair dismissal allegation. Those with greater experience can be challenged by an outsourcing conundrum, within the framework of the latest legislation in this area.

Thus, whatever the reader's level of employment law knowledge, *Human Resources Disputes and Resolutions* enables the reader to accelerate learning greatly. I hope readers find it as useful and enjoyable as we did writing it.

Acknowledgements

I would like to acknowledge the contributions that have been made to *Human Resources Disputes and Resolutions* by the lawyers, HR consultants and support staff over the years:

Seema Barker
Dan Soanes
Roger Greenhalgh
Linda Clark
Emily Blake
Kate Evans
Viv Whatford
Peter Jones
Criona Sproson
Pippa Bennett
Joan Riddell
Paul White
Gareth Kervin
Amanda Poague
Celine Findlay
Sharron Pommels
Lorraine Sherrard
Katie McCarthy
Vikki Hersom
Abi Hanif
Rachael Swindells

About the author

Harry Sherrard is the principal of Sherrards, a leading provider of employment law, HR consultancy and training services to the private, public and voluntary sectors, and has been a specialist employment lawyer for some 15 years. He is recognized as one of the leading employment lawyers in the South East. The Chambers directory, considered the most authoritative in the profession, describes him as 'incredibly well regarded' by clients and fellow lawyers.

Harry covers the full range of employment law work, with a particular speciality in redundancy and restructuring, having managed several large downsizing programmes for clients. More details can be found at www.harrysherrard.com.

He writes and lectures widely on employment law issues and has conducted numerous training programmes for clients throughout London and the South East. He is an adviser to the Shadow DTI team at Westminster, and helps formulate its position on employment law policy.

Harry is well known in the motor racing world, and races an historic Sports 2000 car in the UK and Europe. He is married with three children and lives in rural Sussex.

He also plays bass guitar in the Sherrards rock band.

Chapter 1

Discrimination of various kinds

? Question

Max is the owner of Max Security, a company that employs about 20 people, providing services such as alarm installations. Max is a man with opinions on every subject, opinions which he is not slow to express. Brian has been with the company for about six months, and has gradually adopted a more unconventional appearance, with coloured hair, jewellery and loud clothing. Max dislikes this and teases him endlessly, making sarcastic personal remarks about Brian's appearance in front of other employees. Brian has had enough, resigns, and says he is going to bring legal action against the company for harassment, victimization and bullying.

Can he do this?

Max also has a dislike for vegetarians, and insists that in job advertisements for vacancies at Max Security the words 'Vegetarians need not apply' should be included. This is met with howls of protest from vegetarian would-be applicants, who say they are going to take legal action against Max for this act of blatant discrimination.

Can they do this?

Solution

The words 'discrimination', 'victimization' and 'harassment' are in common usage, and undoubtedly in a general sense Max has indeed been guilty of discrimination, victimization and harassment. In order, however, for any of these concepts to be legally actionable, they must fall under one or more of the anti-harassment Acts. Thus, unless the actions taken by Max are related to the race, sex, disability, sexual orientation, age or religion of the recipient, there is no basis for legal action. In this case, Max's actions, however reprehensible they may be, do not relate to any of these prohibited grounds. It follows that, however aggrieved Brian feels, he is not able to bring legal action for discrimination, victimization or harassment.

Brian has been there for less than a year and so cannot claim unfair dismissal. Had he qualified for unfair dismissal, then he would of course have reasonable grounds for pursuing a constructive dismissal claim.

Generally speaking, 'bullying' is not a free-standing claim. Acts of bullying could form part of a constructive dismissal claim, if the employee has the ability to bring such a claim (ie with over 12 months' service), and if the bullying is connected with any of the prohibited discrimination grounds (as above), then it would form unlawful harassment.

In a very extreme case of bullying, the Protection from Harassment Act 1997 could be relevant. This is intended in the main to give protection to individuals from 'stalkers' and the like, and makes it a criminal offence and also a civil tort to follow a course of conduct (ie two or more acts) which amounts to harassment of another and which the defendant knows, or ought to know, amounts to harassment of another. Harassment is not defined in the Act but includes causing alarm or distress, and conduct is defined as including speech. Notably, the limitation period for such a claim is up to six years, rather than the three months usually applicable in Employment Tribunal cases.

In the 2006 case of *Majrowski* v. *Guy's and St Thomas's NHS Trust*, Mr Majrowski alleged that he was bullied, intimidated and harassed by his line manager. He claimed that she had criticized him excessively, abused him, isolated him and threatened to discipline him if he did not meet (in his eyes unrealistic) targets. The House of Lords decided that Mr Majrowski could hold his employer vicariously liable for the statutory tort of harassment, and that the Act could properly to be applied to employment cases. This case has so far only established the principle that the Protection from Harassment Act can apply in the workplace, and it remains to be seen if on the facts of Mr Majrowski's case he can in fact obtain damages.

Max's conduct here is unlikely to be serious enough to amount to 'harassment' within the meaning of the Act.

In a very extreme case, if bullying resulted in a mental injury, then there could be a personal injury claim. In the well-publicized 2006 case brought by Helen Green against Deutsche Bank, the claimant succeeded in proving that her mental breakdown was caused by the bullying culture at Deutsche Bank, and was awarded £800,000. Widely reported as an 'employment law' case, in fact it was not. Although set in an employment context, the case was a personal injury claim, and the award was met by the Bank's insurers. Nevertheless, it serves as a stark reminder to employers.

In our case, Brian is clearly fed up, but there is no suggestion that he has suffered a mental breakdown, so this type of personal injury claim would not succeed.

With regard to Max's dislike of vegetarians, it has been suggested that vegetarianism might now qualify as a 'philosophical belief', as the Equality Act 2006 defines 'belief' as 'any religious or philosophical belief': it is no longer necessary to show that the belief is similar to a religious belief. If this were accepted, Max may be liable for direct discrimination on grounds of 'philosophical belief'. This point is so far untested.

It may be possible to argue that Max is guilty of indirect discrimination. Indirect discrimination occurs where an across-the-board rule, which impacts one category of employees more than another, is applied. Again, this must be considered in the context of the five unlawful areas. Could the vegetarians construct an argument that a greater proportion of females are vegetarian, or a greater proportion of one religion or another is vegetarian? In order to succeed in these arguments, the employees would have to produce to the Tribunal convincing statistical backup, demonstrating that one religion, or one sex, was adversely impacted by Max's behaviour. Although theoretically possible, in practice such an undertaking is likely to be very difficult.

? Question

The firm's Christmas party was going well until the time came to call for taxis outside the hotel. Timothy is a young, recent recruit, quite mild mannered and shy. He is gay. He attracts the attention of a taxi, which comes over to him. Standing nearby is Linda, the firm's receptionist, and her obnoxious husband, George. George sees the taxi approaching Timothy, very aggressively and rudely moves in front of Timothy, tells Timothy to 'f*** off you poof – this is my taxi', and jumps in. Linda just looks on throughout, and jumps into the taxi with George. The next day Timothy raises a grievance about George's rudeness, bad language, use of insulting comments about his sexuality and general unpleasantness. When Linda is spoken to informally about the events, she says she regrets Timothy was upset, but it was her husband's actions and words, not hers.

Given that George is not your employee, is there anything you can and should do?

Solution

Clearly Timothy has a genuine grievance, and had another employee perpetrated the acts, undoubtedly disciplinary action would be taken. The difficulty here is that Linda was fairly passive, and George is not an employee. It is not advisable to attempt to discipline Linda for the behaviour of her husband.

Past case law in respect of discriminatory language by a third party has come down in favour of protecting the employee. In the 1996 case of *Burton* v. *De Vere Hotels*, two black waitresses at a hotel function had to endure racist remarks from comedian Bernard Manning and the audience. The Employment Appeal Tribunal (EAT) decided that the employer in this case was responsible for allowing racial harassment as the employer had caused or permitted harassment serious enough to amount to a detriment to occur in circumstances in which the employer could control whether it happened or not. It was the element of control that was important, not necessarily whether it was foreseeable.

However, this case is now considered to be very doubtful authority as a result of the 2003 House of Lords judgment in *Macdonald* v. *Advocate-General for Scotland; Pearce* v. *Governing Body of Mayfield Secondary School*. The House of Lords stated that *Burton* v. *De Vere Hotels* was wrongly decided: employers are not vicariously liable for the acts of third parties, and the employer can only be liable for racial discrimination if it would have treated white waitresses better than it treated the black waitresses. So here, your firm will not be guilty of sexual orientation discrimination unless you would have treated a complaint by a heterosexual employee more seriously than Timothy's grievance. Under the circumstances, there does not appear to be much that your firm could have done to protect Timothy from the insulting comments about his sexuality, however unfortunate they may have been.

Under the Health & Safety at Work Act (1974), employers have responsibility for their employees' welfare in the workplace. Under implied terms of an employment contract, specifically the duty of mutual trust and confidence, the employer has duties to maintain a harmonious working environment, and to protect employees against unpleasantness.

A question that arises is whether queuing for taxis outside the hotel following the staff Christmas function is the 'working environment'. Generally speaking, cases have decided that work-related social functions are sufficiently closely connected with work as to come under various rules applying to work and the workplace. It is likely that these events indeed took place in a work environment.

In practical terms, however, it is difficult to know what the firm can do. As stated above, disciplinary action against Linda is unlikely to be justified. Undoubtedly she should be spoken to and the company's unhappiness with the behaviour of her husband should clearly be expressed to her for onward transmission to him. It is probably inappropriate to write or call him directly.

One practical suggestion is to issue general guidance to all employees in respect of forthcoming similar functions, and to state that it is the firm's policy that employees are responsible for the conduct of their guests. That, hopefully, will encourage employees to ensure that their partners behave properly, but it does not change the fundamental position that in the event that a partner does misbehave, disciplinary action against the employee would remain difficult.

Although the firm is unlikely here to want to dismiss Linda, if that line were to be pursued, one possible ground of dismissal which might apply is some other substantial reason. In a very extreme case, if an employee's partner became so problematic that there were many incidents and complaints, the situation could build into one where it might be some other substantial reason to dismiss the spouse.

As far as Timothy is concerned, he is unlikely to be able to claim constructive dismissal as a result of this incident. Constructive dismissal can arise where there is a breach of contract on the part of the employer. As stated above, there are implied terms of mutual trust and confidence, but it is unlikely that this term was breached on this occasion, as the incident was unexpected. Should, however, the firm not take any further action, such as asking Linda to influence the behaviour of her husband and issuing general guidance about the conduct of partners at staff functions, and there was a repeat of this kind of incident, then an employee would have a stronger argument that the employer had failed to comply with the implied term of mutual trust and confidence, which could be the basis for a constructive dismissal.

DISCRIMINATION – SEX

Question

Sarah has always had a poor attendance record, regularly taking two or three days off each month, often giving 'period pains' as the reason. Just over six months ago she began a spell of absence which is still continuing. It has been certified as for endometriosis.

She has now exhausted her company sick pay entitlement and you recently asked her (in accordance with your normal practice after such a long absence) to visit your company doctor – who also obtained, with Sarah's consent, a report from Sarah's own doctor. Your doctor's report says that Sarah is unlikely to be fit enough to return to work in the near future: the pain, lethargy and general tiredness which have rendered her unfit for work over the past few months have not so far been abated by medication and there seems little likelihood of that changing. The only certain cure for her condition is a complete hysterectomy, which she is unwilling to undergo until all other treatments have been tried and failed as she still hopes to have children. Even if she were willing to undergo the operation, there is a long waiting list and it would leave her incapable of work for a considerable period.

In discussing that medical report with her, you said that you could not keep her job open indefinitely. She replied, 'but you can't sack me for this, it would be sex discrimination'.

Is she right?

Solution

No, she is not. Direct sex discrimination against a woman occurs when 'on the ground of her sex [an employer] treats her less favourably than [it] treats or would treat a man'. Any dismissal in this case would not – on its face at least – be 'on the ground of' Sarah's sex.

The Employment Equality (Sex Discrimination) Regulations 2005 amended the Sex Discrimination Act 1975 (SDA) to make it absolutely clear that discrimination on grounds of pregnancy or maternity leave is sex discrimination. Dismissal for a reason which is *pregnancy*-related is 'on the ground' of a woman's sex. An employer cannot argue that it would have treated a man (who was absent through illness for a similar length of time) the same. The law requires that any comparison for this purpose 'must be such that the relevant circumstances in the one case are the same, or not materially different, in the other'. Pregnancy is a natural condition, not an illness. It can only ever apply to women. So the circumstances can never be the same for a man.

Although pregnancy is not an illness, it can cause illness. To the extent that any such illness disables a woman during pregnancy or the period allowed by law for maternity leave, it is treated as being 'pregnancy-related'. The SDA now provides that 'where a person's treatment of a woman is on grounds of illness suffered by the woman as a consequence of pregnancy, that treatment is to be taken to be on the ground of the pregnancy'. However, this is limited to the protected period. An employer who dismisses because of such an absence, or takes it into account in assessing the woman's total amount of absence when more generally considering dismissal on grounds of capability, will indeed be discriminating 'on the ground' of sex. Outside that specially protected period, however, the law ceases to treat an illness as 'pregnancy-related' even if it had its basis in pregnancy. It then becomes just an 'illness'. Men, like women, can be 'ill'. So it is then permissible for an employer to argue that it would have treated a man who was absent through illness for a similar length of time the same.

However, the fact that endometriosis is to do with a woman's reproductive organs does not make it 'pregnancy-related'. The fact that it is sex-specific to females does not mean that no valid comparison can be made with a man. Men, too, suffer from sex-specific illnesses (eg prostate problems).

That Sarah is wrong on the sex discrimination point does not, of course, necessarily mean that you can dismiss her and that it will be fair. A person with a medical condition which has a substantial long-term effect on his or her ability to undertake normal day-to-day activities (as it seems might well be the case with Sarah) is protected by the Disability Discrimination Act (1995) (DDA). You may, therefore, be under a duty to see whether any 'reasonable adjustments' could be made so as to overcome any disadvantages in Sarah's employment that arise from the disability from which she suffers. Having said that, it is difficult to see how altering her job, or her hours, or seeking alternative work for Sarah could have any effect here. It does not seem that there is any aspect of the job or conditions which is placing her under any disadvantage. It is just that she is not fit to do any work at all.

You will also, if you are to proceed to dismissal, need to ensure that it is 'reasonable' – eg consistent with how you would treat anyone else, male or female, with a similar length of absence and prognosis – and handled in accordance with the statutory Dismissal and Disciplinary Procedures.

DISCRIMINATION – SEX AND RACE

? Question

Bodgit & Co have a discretionary bonus which is paid to all its employees every February. In January, Malik raises a grievance about racial harassment against some of his colleagues. In February he is the only member of his team not to be awarded a bonus.

The MD insists this is contractually acceptable because the bonus is always only discretionary. Another member of his team is also from an ethnic minority, so the MD says he cannot have a racial discrimination claim.

How do you advise?

Solution

Section 2 of the Race Relations Act 1976 makes victimization a separate and distinct head of claim. Victimization occurs when someone (the victim) is treated less favourably than others are or would be treated in the same circumstances because the discriminator knows, believes or suspects that the victim has brought or intends to bring proceedings under the Race Relations Act, give evidence under any proceedings under the Act, do anything in relation to the Race Relations Act or allege that someone has committed an act which would amount to a contravention of the Act.

Malik has raised a grievance about racial harassment against some of his work colleagues and, since the allegations of racial harassment are acts of discrimination under the Race Relations Act 1976, Malik is protected from the less favourable treatment which he receives as a result of bringing this grievance.

To some extent, any allegations of victimization would be dependent on other circumstances. Where the bonus is discretionary, there may be particular factors which are considered when giving out the bonus. For example, if the bonus is calculated on a team effort and Malik is the only person not to be given a bonus, it would appear that the only reason could be victimization. However, where the bonus may be calculated on individual performance and it can be shown that Malik has performed poorly in comparison to everybody else, there may be a possible argument for not awarding him such a bonus.

However, the burden of proof in racial discrimination cases, like other forms of discrimination, now require that once Malik has 'proved facts from which a Tribunal could conclude an act of discrimination has taken place', the burden of proof will shift to the employer, to show that the treatment was 'in no sense whatsoever' on grounds of race. In *Barton* v. *Investec Henderson Crossthwaite Securities* (2003) the Court of Appeal laid down important guidelines on the burden of proof, in a case involving a female manager who had been given less favourable non-contractual bonuses. If the employer does not have a clear, transparent system for awarding bonuses, it may be difficult for it to satisfy this requirement.

In respect of the MD's insistence that the bonus is discretionary and so the company is entitled to do whatever it likes, this raises other issues in addition to racial harassment. In a High Court case, *Clark* v. *Nomura*

(2002), the employee's contract stated that the bonus was discretionary and not guaranteed in any way … 'and is dependent on individual performance'. Mr Clark earned bonuses of £1.75 million and £800,000 in previous years. He was dismissed by his employer owing to a loss of confidence, inappropriate dress and appearance, erratic attendance and timekeeping and his criticism of management in front of peers and subordinates. The employer did not pay his bonus for that year and argued that it could exercise its discretion in this way, despite the fact that he had earned large profits for the company in the preceding year. The High Court disagreed, and awarded Mr Clark a bonus of £1.35 million. The High Court concluded that 'an employer exercising a discretion which on the face of it is unfettered or absolute will be in breach of contract if no reasonable employer would have exercised discretion in that way'. In these circumstances their judgment was based on the fact that Mr Clark was employed to earn profits and as he did earn profits, it was perverse and unlawful not to award him a bonus. An employer's discretion in these circumstances is not without limitations.

Question

Mr DeNiro, an Italian with only a moderate grasp of the English language, was employed as a butcher in a large supermarket, working behind the meat counter with three other butchers.

The supermarket decided it needed one of the four butchers to act as supervisor, one of these tasks being to write weekly reports on the amount and types of meat sold. Mr DeNiro applied for the job and was suitable in most respects for the promotion, but was not offered it owing to his poor grasp of English.

Mr DeNiro thinks that the supermarket should have provided him with English language classes which would have allowed him to do the job.

Would Mr DeNiro succeed in a discrimination claim?

Solution

Mr DeNiro could pursue a claim of indirect discrimination under the Race Relations Act. The employer imposed a requirement that the supervisor in the department had to have a good grasp of English, and so Mr DeNiro would argue that this is indirect discrimination because it is to the detriment of all non-English races. Unlike direct discrimination, indirect discrimination can be justified (see below). Mr DeNiro will therefore have to argue and convince the Tribunal that the requirement to have a high standard of English is not justified, whilst the employer will have to show that the requirement was justified.

In basic terms, justification will be proven by showing that the requirement for good English related to a real business need. If there is no such need for the supervisor to have such a good grasp of English language to write the weekly reports, then it is unlikely that the employer will be able to justify the discrimination shown. For example, if the weekly reports are based mainly on numbers and products, and Mr DeNiro would have been able to write such reports, then his standard of English would be sufficient to be able to work as the supervisor. In other words, Mr DeNiro would succeed if the employer had not imposed a standard of English inappropriately high for the job in question. That is not to say that employers are not entitled to require specific levels of written and spoken English; they are, but the standards imposed must realistically match the requirements of the job.

Another aspect of justification to be considered is that since Mr DeNiro is willing to take classes in bringing his grasp of the English language to a higher standard, is the supermarket chain justified in not having waited until he had completed or at least started these classes? Is the employer justified in not paying for courses? The answers to these questions depend on the facts and circumstances, but generally employers facing immediate business needs are entitled to proceed, and are not required to delay unduly. Paying for a course for Mr DeNiro would set a precedent in the minds of other employees, and the employer is likely to be justified in taking the position that all employees need to be treated equally.

❓ Question

Fly Shanghai is a new Chinese airline taking advantage of the growing Chinese economy and trade between Europe and China. It flies routes between Shanghai and Heathrow, and primarily caters for Chinese businessmen, officials and tourists travelling to and from London. Fly Shanghai decides to set up a London base for cabin crew, and in advertisements placed in UK publications, the following stipulations are included: 'All applicants must be fluent in either Cantonese or Mandarin. All applicants must be at least 5' 4" tall.'

What issues might arise from these recruitment procedures?

Solution !

1. Obviously, the vast majority of people who speak fluent Cantonese or Mandarin are Chinese. Therefore, the policy of recruiting only speakers of these languages appears to discriminate against all other races. The requirement to speak Cantonese or Mandarin is a condition or requirement imposed by the employer, which has a disproportionate impact on a particular group of potential applicants, ie non-Chinese. It appears, therefore, on the face of it to be an act of indirect racial discrimination. However, indirect discrimination can be justified. The justification here is that the majority of Fly Shanghai's passengers are ethnic Chinese and therefore, from the point of view of customer service and health and safety, it is appropriate that cabin crew speak the language of their passengers. It is, therefore, likely that the indirect discrimination will be justified, and therefore not unlawful.

2. Men on the whole are taller than women and therefore (although we doubt if any statistics actually exist) it is arguably sex discrimination against women to impose a 5' 4" height restriction. More women than men will probably be shorter than that, so it is a similar disproportionate impact analysis as set out above, which could then lead to indirect sex discrimination. However, the minimum height requirement is entirely imposed for health and safety reasons and is therefore certainly justified.

3. Similarly, height restrictions are also likely to be indirectly discriminatory on racial grounds, as members of certain racial groups are statistically shorter than other racial groups. The Metropolitan Police force, for example, changed their minimum height requirements in order to recruit more members of ethnic minority groups. But again, the key question is whether the height requirement is justified, on health and safety grounds.

Question

Martha is the best-qualified applicant for a job in George's department – and she is also his wife. You have no formal policy about partners working together but are worried that it may produce problems.

Should you reject Martha's application?

Solution

This raises potential issues concerning sex discrimination, and discrimination against married people. Discrimination against married people is specifically prohibited by the Sex Discrimination Act 1975. In the 2002 case of *Chief Constable of the Bedfordshire Constabulary* v. *Graham*, a woman police inspector's appointment to a divisional post was rescinded by the chief constable on the grounds that her husband – a chief superintendent – was the commander of that division. His major reason was his view that as the spouse of a serving officer, she should not work in the same division because she would not be a competent and compellable witness against her spouse in any criminal proceedings. As this was direct discrimination against a married person, the chief constable could not justify it.

He also considered that it would be difficult for officers under her supervision to make a complaint or take a grievance knowing of her relationship with a divisional commander, and it would be more difficult to deal with any possible problems relating to underperformance by her because of her relationship with a divisional commander. An Employment Tribunal held that this constituted indirect sex discrimination, as a considerably higher proportion of women police officers were married to male police officers than male police officers were married to women in the force. The chief constable had failed to justify the policy. It was also both direct and indirect (again unjustified) discrimination on grounds of marital status. The EAT rejected appeals against all those findings.

So far as indirect discrimination (on grounds of both sex and marital status) is concerned, your circumstances might be sufficiently different from those of the Bedfordshire Constabulary that a decision might go the other way. Perhaps the make-up of your staff is such that – unlike in that case – such a policy might not impact unequally on men and women. Or, even if there was a disparate impact, you might – unlike the employer in that case – be able to justify it by showing that it was a proportionate way of meeting a real business need. However, this would seem unlikely. You have no evidence that employing Martha will actually produce any problems, and if it did, then you should deal with those problems appropriately.

Further, if any policy, practice or specific decision rested purely on marital status – that is, if you stopped wives working with husbands, or husbands working with wives, but did not stop unmarried people working together even though they were in some sort of close relationship – that would be direct discrimination contrary to s.3(1)(a) of the Sex

Discrimination Act 1975. That says 'a person discriminates against a married person of either sex if [...] on the ground of his or her marital status he treats that person less favourably than he treats or would treat an unmarried person of the same sex'. And there can be no justification of direct discrimination.

It is also possible that you would face a claim for sex discrimination: but for her sex, Martha would not have been married to George, and would not have been refused employment. If you want to avoid such claims, it would be better to have a clear policy against intimate relationships between employees, or applicants for employment and existing employees, and implement this policy in a non-discriminatory way, to men and women alike.

? Question

You and Melanie are old school friends and she is a team leader at the company where you work.

Over a drink one night she tells you that the male regional director has made some sexually harassing comments to her, the least offensive of which is that she will definitely get a promotion if she continues to wear 'those cute little skirts'. She insists that you must not take any further action or tell anyone.

What do you do?

Solution **!**

This is a difficult situation for you as you have been given information regarding sexual harassment and asked not to take this any further, not simply by another work colleague, but also an old friend of yours. However, at the same time your friend should appreciate that as you have management responsibilities, she puts you in a difficult position by asking you not to take any further action. If a director is behaving in a way that could be seen as harassment, it is unlikely that it is only your friend who is affected: you may find that the director is subjecting other women to such comments, and there may even be incidents of physical harassment.

The Sex Discrimination Act 1975 was amended from 1 October 2005 so that harassment is now specifically defined. There are two types of harassment under the new SDA: harassment on grounds of sex, and sexual harassment.

A person subjects a woman to harassment if, on grounds of her sex, he engages in unwanted conduct that has the purpose or effect of: (i) violating her dignity; or (ii) creating an intimidating, hostile, degrading, humiliating or offensive environment for her. There is no longer any specific need to compare how the person would have treated a man, but the conduct does need to be because of the woman's sex, and not for some other reason.

Sexual harassment occurs when a person engages in any form of unwanted verbal, non-verbal or physical conduct of a sexual nature which has the purpose or effect of: (i) violating her dignity; or (ii) creating an intimidating, hostile, degrading, humiliating or offensive environment for her. Employers are vicariously liable for the acts of their employees unless they can show that they took such steps as were reasonably practicable to prevent the employee from carrying out the acts in respect of which the complaint is made.

If you do not take any action, in circumstances where the employer is aware of what is happening, and later the employer is taken to a Tribunal for unlawful sex discrimination, it would be difficult, if not impossible, to show that the company did everything it could to avoid sexual harassment of its employees.

The best solution here would be for you to talk Melanie round and explain that other employees may be suffering from sexual harassment, and if she allows you to investigate the situation, it may help a lot of people. If she continues to refuse, you have a dilemma, but the most advisable course of action from a legal point of view is to inform Melanie that she has given you information in respect of which you have no alternative but to act, in the interests of the employer and all its employees. This will not do much for your friendship with Melanie, but you have duties to your employer.

However, where there is a compelling reason not to do so, and Melanie does persuade you in some way not to take any action, then it would be prudent to make a note of the conversation that you had with Melanie to expressly state that she insisted that you take no further action and, under your duty to her, you felt an obligation not to do so. This will at least protect you from a situation in the future where Melanie alleges that you should have taken action.

Another suggestion is to have some general guidance and training on sexual harassment in the company, and to use this to inform the director (indirectly) that his conduct is not appropriate. The introduction of the new law on sexual harassment in 2005 provides a good opportunity to review existing policies, and make sure they comply with the new provisions.

Employers should have an anti-harassment policy and procedure, which, amongst other things, provides that complainants making complaints in good faith will not be penalized in any way.

? Question

Several members of the sales team employed by Grafter and Slack would meet regularly every Friday evening after work, at a nearby pub, for a drink.

Grafter and Slack manufactured and sold beauty products, and although it did have a small range designed specifically for men, the majority of its clients, and indeed sales staff, were female.

Colin has recently joined the sales team, and was coerced into attending the Friday night session with his colleagues, during which remarks of a sexual nature were made directly to him by two of his female colleagues. Colin was shocked and offended by this behaviour and reported the matter, in writing, to his manager the following Monday morning. She told him that it was harmless banter and not to take offence.

If he resigned, would Colin have a constructive dismissal and/or discrimination claim?

Solution !

The possible claim that Colin would have against Grafter and Slack would be constructive dismissal and sex discrimination. Following the amendments to the Sex Discrimination Act in October 2005, there is now a specific wrong of sexual harassment, which is deemed to be a form of sex discrimination. Sexual harassment occurs when a person engages in any form of unwanted verbal, non-verbal or physical conduct of a sexual nature which has the purpose or effect of: (i) violating his or her dignity; or (ii) creating an intimidating, hostile, degrading, humiliating or offensive environment for him or her.

There is no need to show that the reason for the conduct was because the victim was a woman (or a man): sexual conduct that violates dignity etc will be harassment even where men and women were equally treated. The statements made to Colin are clearly sexual, and they have also had the effect of violating his dignity and creating an intimidatory atmosphere.

Employers can be vicariously liable for the actions of their employees, unless they are able to use the defence that they 'took such steps as were reasonably practicable to prevent the employee from doing that act'. Whether or not they could have stopped the act taking place is dependent on the circumstances, and the Tribunal will look at whether they have an anti-harassment and anti-bullying policy and whether they have an equal opportunities policy. The Tribunal will also look at whether any such instances have occurred in the past and whether the employer has failed to act on them. The Tribunal will look very seriously at the fact that when it has come to their attention (assuming that it has not before) they have not taken any action and dismissed it as merely 'harmless banter'.

With regard to the constructive dismissal claim, the fact that they are not taking any action could be seen as a fundamental breach of contract, and it could also be seen that as Colin has raised this in writing, they are refusing to deal with a grievance in the proper way. Since October 2004, the failure to follow the statutory grievance procedure (by not holding a meeting etc) would make this an automatically unfair dismissal. However, as Colin has only recently joined the company, he may not have sufficient service to claim constructive unfair dismissal. Nevertheless, if the company is found liable for sex discrimination, as seems likely, the failure to follow the statutory grievance procedure can lead to an increase in compensation for sex discrimination by up to 50 per cent.

In respect of the issue that the remarks that were made to Colin were made at a pub, and during an event which was not formally organized by the employer, this would still be considered 'in the course of employment' as has been found by the case of *Chief Constable of Lincolnshire Police* v. *Stubbs* (1999). In this case one of the incidents of inappropriate sexual behaviour was at a leaving party. However, the other incident was when the complainant went to the pub where she met other police officers; this was not a social event organized by the employers. At the pub a male colleague pulled up his pub stool close to the complainant, flicked her hair and rearranged her collar, giving the impression there was a relationship between them. The Employment Appeal Tribunal found that this was in the course of employment and that sexual harassment had occurred.

Question

Samantha has just been recruited as a secretary by an old traditional firm of criminal lawyers situated near to the Old Bailey in London. She is told on her first day that the firm has a dress code which requires ladies to wear dresses and not trousers and gentlemen to wear navy or black suits.

Samantha is disgusted by this and so on the second day turns up to work in a trouser suit. She is immediately sent home by her superior and told to come back to work in a skirt.

Samantha thinks she may have a sex discrimination claim. Does she have a claim and is she likely to succeed?

Solution !

If Samantha did have a sex discrimination claim it would be for direct discrimination under the Sex Discrimination Act based on the fact that women are being treated less favourably than men because, in this instance, women are not allowed to wear trousers to work, solely because they are women.

The general rule on dress codes is that where there are restrictions on dress for both sexes, an employer will not be in breach of the Sex Discrimination Act. The authority is *Schmidt* v. *Austicks Bookshops Ltd* (1997) where the Employment Appeal Tribunal held that where uniform requirements are imposed on both sexes, discrimination is not established just because these requirements are different. Judge Phillips stated that it is better to look at these issues as questions of 'uniform', rather than on a 'garment by garment' basis.

In the case of *Burritt* v. *West Birmingham Health Authority* (1994), it was held that just because an employee honestly believes that she has been treated less favourably does not of itself establish less favourable treatment. It is for the Employment Tribunal alone to decide whether there has been any less favourable treatment by applying an objective test. It does not matter that Samantha is disgusted by the dress code, as the Tribunal would decide by applying an objective test as to whether the dress code did amount to 'less favourable treatment'.

In *Department for Work and Pensions* v. *Thompson* (2004), the EAT upheld a dress code which required men to wear a collar and tie, as an equivalent level of smartness was demanded of women members of staff.

In these circumstances therefore, as the employer was imposing a dress code on both sexes, in that men were only allowed to wear particular coloured suits and women were only allowed to wear skirts or dresses, an Employment Tribunal may conclude that there is no sex discrimination. The fact that this particular case relates to a formal environment aids the employer.

However, the tide may have turned against employers on the women in trousers issue. Trousers are now widely seen as acceptable dress, and in a number of cases it has been accepted that 'dresses only' can amount to sex discrimination. In *Owen* v. *Professional Golf Association* (2000), a woman won her case where the employer had sent her home to change when she came to work in a smart trouser suit, the Equal Opportunities Commission (EOC) won a settlement in a case brought by a schoolgirl who wasn't allowed to wear trousers, and female Eurostar guards won a dispute over trousers at work.

On a slightly different note, but of equal interest, in the case of *Smith* v. *Safeway Plc* (1996) the Court of Appeal held that it was not unlawful sex discrimination where a male employee had been dismissed for having long hair. The conclusion was that a dress or grooming code that aims to achieve a conventional appearance will not be discriminatory, even though it requires different standards for men and women. Whether an employer has authority to require an employee to cut his hair is a different question to whether that is an act of sex discrimination; and whether an employer has authority to dismiss an employee for not cutting his hair is a different question again.

? Question

Chris and Penny have been married for seven years and have three children under five. After each child Penny has gone back to work full time.

Neither Chris nor Penny is very happy with their current childcare arrangements and Penny has decided that she would like to reduce her hours from full- to part-time.

Penny's employer, however, has told her that she cannot work on a part-time basis and Penny has resigned and is claiming discrimination. Would her claim be successful?

Solution

Following her maternity leave, Penny has a statutory right to return to the job in which she was employed, on terms and conditions which are not less favourable than they would have been had she not been away on maternity leave. She does not have a statutory right to insist on returning to work on a part-time basis.

Regardless of any statutory right, however, Penny may be able to claim indirect sex discrimination in that her employer is applying a criterion, ie the necessity to work full-time, which will affect a considerably larger proportion of women than men. It will then be for her employer to show that the refusal to allow her to work part-time was justified. If the decision not to allow Penny to return can be objectively justified on the grounds that there was a genuine business reason to employ only a full-timer, then Penny will not succeed. In persuading an Employment Tribunal of this, an employer would have to show that it considered Penny's request seriously and did not dismiss it out of hand. It would be helpful if it was able to show, in writing, what its thought process had been and, for example, show meetings between HR and line managers and colleagues where the possibilities of reduced hours and/or job shares were discussed. The argument that the employer has a policy against job shares, or that job share arrangements increase administrative costs and hassle, would be unlikely to be a genuine business reason in defeating a discrimination claim.

Penny also has a right to request flexible working for the purposes of carrying out childcare responsibilities, as indeed does Chris. This applies with respect to children under the age of six, and will be extended in the future to workers with caring responsibilities for adults, such as elderly parents. The request should be made in writing, and the employer then has to follow a set procedure in considering the request, and can only reject the request on certain business-related grounds.

Question

Sales staff have personal targets and each gets an annual bonus calculated with reference to how he or she performed against that target. You receive an equal pay questionnaire from the only woman in the sales team asking what each man's target, performance and bonus were for the year just completed.

How do you respond?

Solution

The equal pay questionnaire – in a similar form to that already in use under the Sex Discrimination Act and the Race Relations Act – was introduced on 6 April 2003 by the Equal Pay (Questions and Replies) Order 2003. It does not expressly cover a request for the sort of information asked for here. It allows a person to say that he or she believes that he or she is not being paid equally with a person of the opposite sex and to ask the employer for an acknowledgement that that is so or, if not, for an explanation of why the employer believes it is not so or of any difference that does exist. An employer has eight weeks in which to reply. If a case is subsequently brought, a Tribunal is entitled to draw any inference that it wishes from a failure to reply within that time period, or from an evasive or equivocal reply, including the inference that the employer was in breach of the Equal Pay Act. So you would be wise to reply to this questionnaire.

It may – despite the absence of a specific requirement on you to provide information in the form and detail requested – sometimes be in an employer's interest in answering such questions to provide specific factual information. Against that, however, have to be balanced the rights of the male employees about whom the information is sought. It is quite likely that divulging such information in a form which can be traced back to specific individuals would involve breach of the Data Protection Act or of some contractual duty of confidentiality. One way round that would be to seek each individual's specific consent to the disclosure, but you may not wish to do that and, even if you did, it may not be granted.

Another route might be to 'anonymize' the information – that is, give figures without identifying which figures related to which employee – but where a small number of employees are involved it might be easy for a person with some knowledge of the working situation to identify individuals even without their names being given. If a case were ever brought to a Tribunal, issues like these would probably be dealt with in preliminary hearings. Tribunals can make orders about disclosure of documents and any such orders would override the individuals' rights under the Data Protection Act. At this stage, however, such rights remain live.

So your reply should be restricted to answering, in specific terms, the specific questions that are asked on the questionnaire. In so far as you can do so without breaching other employees' rights, you may wish to provide some or all of the specific additional information requested. If you are unwilling or unable to do this, you should say why.

? Question

You are interviewing for a female residential social worker in a home for elderly women. The applicant's name was 'Patricia' but clearly when 'Patricia' turned up for interview she very much resembled a man. 'Patricia' explained that her real name is 'Patrick' but she was currently undergoing gender reassignment.

Can you refuse Patrick's application on the grounds that 'she's a 'he'?

Solution !

The Sex Discrimination (Gender Reassignment) Regulations 1999 amended the Sex Discrimination Act 1975 to make it discriminatory to subject a person to less favourable treatment on the grounds that they: '... intend to undergo, is undergoing or has undergone gender reassignment' (section 2A SDA). Therefore, in the normal course of events, an employer should not allow this turn of events to affect the recruitment process.

However, in the current case, it is possible that a position of 'resident social worker' in a home for elderly women may fall within 'genuine occupational qualification' (GOQ) exceptions set out in section 7B of the SDA, which provides that employers may be able to apply the GOQ requirements in the context of gender reassignment where 'the holder of the job provides vulnerable individuals with personal services promoting their welfare, or similar personal services, and in the reasonable view of the employer those services cannot be effectively provided by a person whilst that person is undergoing gender reassignment'. The key issue will be whether it is reasonable for the employer to take that view.

Also, the Gender Recognition Act 2004 gives legal recognition to the acquired gender where transsexual people satisfy the Gender Recognition Panel that they

- have or have had gender dysphoria;
- have lived in the acquired gender for two years;
- intend to live permanently in the acquired gender.

If Patrick has a full gender recognition certificate, the GOQ exception does not apply: legally, Patrick is a woman.

See also pages 49 and 103.

DISCRIMINATION – RELIGION OR BELIEF

Question

You have an employee, Barbara, in the insurance department who belongs to the British National Party, and has expressed 'white supremacy' views. Barbara is claiming that because of the 'new law' that's come into force she is able to share her 'beliefs' with anyone she wants and that you can't prevent her from talking to her colleagues about her opinions, however extreme they may be.

You are concerned that Barbara's 'beliefs' may potentially lead the company into having to defend a race discrimination claim. Are you able to restrict Barbara in the expression of her 'beliefs'?

Solution

Barbara is referring to the Employment Equality (Religion or Belief) Regulations 2003 that came into force in 2003 and were updated in 2006. The Regulations make it unlawful to discriminate against an individual for following a particular religion or belief.

The definition within the Regulations originally referred to 'religion, religious belief or similar philosophical belief', but was amended in 2006 so as to remove the requirement that a philosophical belief has to be 'similar to' a religious belief.

In *Baggs* v. *Fudge* (2006), an Employment Tribunal rejected a claim from a BNP member that they had been discriminated against because of a religious or philosophical belief, but it is arguable that the new definition may make it easier for members of political parties to claim protection. Also, in *Refearn* v. *Serco* (2006), the Court of Appeal held that the dismissal of a BNP member was not unlawful as it was not 'on racial grounds', despite the employee arguing that since he had to be white to be in the BNP, the dismissal was on the grounds of his race.

The issue here is not what views Barbara holds per se, but how she is voicing them within the workplace. By voicing her opinions, Barbara risks a race discrimination claim being brought not only against herself but also against the company, and therefore action needs to be taken to address this before any serious issues arise. If Barbara is expressing racist views, this may well amount to harassing behaviour in respect of other employees.

The concept of vicarious liability means that the company is likely to be liable for any discriminatory acts Barbara takes during the course of her employment. Within your contracts and handbooks there should exist a policy on discrimination, which should include a provision for invoking the disciplinary procedure in situations where employees breach the policy. Barbara should be reminded of this policy and advised that any breach could result in disciplinary action being taken against her, including dismissal. It will also help to advise Barbara that not only can a claim be brought against the company for race discrimination but one can also be brought against her as an individual.

By stopping Barbara from expressing those beliefs within a secular workplace you are not restricting her right to hold those beliefs, but simply restricting how she voices her opinions to others. You should ensure that all employees are advised of the same policy to avoid claims of discrimination on the grounds of religion or belief.

Question

A Muslim manager has admonished a female member of his staff for wearing short skirts and about the fact that she lives with her partner before marriage. She has brought a complaint of sex discrimination against him. You discuss the allegation with the manager, but he says he feels you are discriminating against him by disciplining him for expressing his religious views.

Does either of them have a claim and how would you deal with this situation?

Solution !

The Employment Equality (Religion or Belief) Regulations 2003 came into force on 2 December 2003, and although now in force for three years, not that many cases have worked their way through the Tribunal system.

In brief précis the purpose of the Religion or Belief Regulations is to prevent an employer from subjecting its employees to direct or indirect discrimination in the workplace on the grounds of the employee's religion or belief. This covers both direct and indirect discrimination, victimization and harassment, which is defined as: 'violating dignity or creating an intimidating, hostile, degrading, humiliating or offensive environment'.

Clearly, if the employer in the current situation were disciplining the manager on the grounds, for example, that he was taking regular prayer breaks then this may fall directly within the Regulations. However, the disciplinary action is being taken because the manager is attempting to impose his religious values on a female member of staff who, presumably, does not share those values.

The Regulations were amended in 2006 to make it clear that any reference to religion also includes lack of religion, and this now protects employees who are discriminated against because they do not share the particular religion of the discriminator. So you could be vicariously liable for the discriminatory conduct of the manager against the female member of staff, on the grounds of her lack of Muslim belief.

Further, the manager's behaviour may also be sex discriminatory. The manager's comment about 'living with a partner before marriage' is arguably sex neutral (the same comment could have been made to a man) and so would not constitute sex discrimination. However, the comment about 'short skirts' is clearly sex based and may lead to a successful claim of sex discrimination from the female employee. She can bring a claim directly against the Muslim manager, and also against the employer, through the principle of vicarious liability.

We would suggest that the manager is not being discriminated against for being a Muslim but, rather, attempting to impose Muslim values in a secular workplace. The Regulations are intended to allow people to hold and practise religious beliefs but, we suspect, not to the extent of being allowed to proselytize or impose those views or practices on others. However, there is still little guidance from the courts on these matters.

? Question

Sally is the assistant HR officer at Global Tours and, following a life-changing Tibetan holiday last summer, has become a Buddhist.

Global Tours operates a compulsory four-day shutdown over Christmas, which has to be taken as part of annual leave. However, Sally insists that she wants to continue working over the Christmas period, and will, instead, take four days off during the year to coincide with various Buddhist celebrations. Sally maintains that she cannot be made to recognize Christmas, which is a Christian holiday, when she is a Buddhist.

Can you force Sally to observe the four-day Christmas shutdown?

Solution

The Employment Equality (Religion or Belief) Regulations 2003 make it unlawful to discriminate against employees because of their religion or belief. Religion is defined broadly, and would certainly include Buddhism. But it will not necessarily be unlawful discrimination to insist Sally takes time off over Christmas.

First, any employer can set specific times when workers can take their leave under the Working Time Regulations. Employers are required to give notice if there is a specified period when employees must take their holiday and this is a period which is twice the length of the period that the annual leave will be. So in these circumstances the Christmas shutdown is for four days and the employer is therefore required under the Working Time Regulations to give eight days' notice. As long as the employer has complied with the notice period under the Working Time Regulations, there is no reason why Sally cannot be forced to observe the shutdown at Christmas regardless of the fact that it is a Christian celebration.

It could be argued that Buddhists are being treated less favourably than Christians as the Christmas shutdown is a recognized holiday for Christians, and Christians receive this holiday, whereas Buddhist employees do not automatically have leave at the time of their festivals. Our view is, however, that as Sally is being treated in the same way as other employees, there is no direct discrimination here on grounds of her religion. The business is closed down at Christmas. It is because of that closure, rather than religion per se, that the company insists that she takes leave then. Clearly it is impractical for many reasons for her to work on her own over the Christmas shutdown period.

As far as indirect discrimination is concerned, it may be argued by Sally that requiring her to take leave at Christmas, or refusing her time off for various Buddhist festivals, does amount to indirect discrimination. The key question here will be whether the employer can justify its decision: the employer needs to show there is a legitimate aim, and that the practice is proportionate to that aim. So it is almost certainly justifiable to close the business for four days over Christmas, but it may be harder to justify refusing Sally time off for Buddhist festivals, providing she gives reasonable notice etc.

See also page 85.

DISCRIMINATION – DISABILITY

Question

You employ staff to work in a dusty factory, where breathing equipment is mandatory. An employee develops a severe chest problem. He wants to carry on, but you are concerned about his health and safety.

Should you let him continue working?

Solution

1. This could be said to be a reversal of the normal situation where an employee goes off sick and a capability dismissal is contemplated in the context of that employee's absence. In this situation the employee is continuing to come to work, but appears not to be medically fit to do so. Capability is, however, not necessarily linked to absence, and therefore you are able to progress a capability dismissal based on the individual's health and ability to do the job, even though he is currently attending work. Therefore, if you do want to move towards a dismissal, capability will be the primary fair reason. In addition, the fair dismissal reason of 'some other substantial reason' may be relevant in circumstances where the dismissal is essentially for the employee's own good. Further, some other substantial reason may apply where dismissal will prevent the employer from being exposed to litigation (see point 4 below).

   However, in *Coxall* v. *Goodyear Great Britain Ltd* (2002) the Court of Appeal confirmed that there is no legal duty on an employer to dismiss an employee who wants to go on working merely because there is some risk to the employee, as the employee is free to decide what risks he or she wishes to take (the principle laid down in *Whither*

v. *Perry Chain Co Ltd* in 1961). Although employers' health and safety responsibilities are much stricter now, society's increasing respect for individual autonomy is a countervailing consideration. But every case depends upon its own facts: there will certainly be cases where the employer will be under a duty to dismiss the employee for his own good, or to protect him from physical danger, despite the fact that the employee wishes to go on working.

2.   The severe chest problem could well be a disability. First, the employer needs to consider whether this is a physical impairment which is likely to have a substantial long-term adverse effect on the employee's normal day-to-day activities. Remember that the effect of the disability is largely assessed in the employee's everyday life, rather than his work life. Therefore, if an illness affects the employee only at work, but he is able to lead a completely normal life outside of work, he does not qualify as disabled under the DDA. Here the condition is described as a severe chest problem, so the chances are that the breathing activities are going to have a detrimental effect on his abilities, such as mobility, or lifting or moving everyday objects. The condition may also qualify as a disability, even if it does not yet have a substantial adverse effect on his everyday life, if the medical evidence shows that it is likely to have such an effect in the future.

It is possible to dismiss a disabled employee without him being able to bring a successful DDA claim against the employer if that dismissal is justified. The justification in a case such as this is simply that the employee cannot do his job for a reason relating to disability. Before arriving at a dismissal decision, the employer must consider reasonable adjustments. The rules in this area were strengthened on 1 October 2004, and an employer will have no answer to a DDA claim if it has not considered reasonable adjustments. Obvious examples of reasonable adjustments in this case would be air conditioning and breathing apparatus, but the concept extends to other aspects of employment and would include variations of his job, including perhaps a transfer to an office-based job, if one is available, and if he has the ability to undertake that job with a moderate amount of training.

3.   Under the Health & Safety at Work Act and related Regulations, employers are responsible for the health, safety and welfare of their employees. Exposing an employee to dust where he has a severe chest problem, and where further injury could result, could lead to a prosecution by the Health & Safety Executive. Just because the employee has said he wants to carry on does not prevent the employer being potentially liable to such a prosecution.

4. The employee could also sue the organization for personal injury if his condition deteriorates as a result of the dust. Damages could be awarded if a deterioration is measurable as a result of exposure to the dust, although clearly in this case it is not suggested that the employer is responsible for the original condition. However, in *Hatton* v. *Sutherland* (2002), the Court of Appeal said that if the only reasonable and effective step would have been to dismiss or demote the employee, the employer would not be in breach of duty in allowing a willing employee to continue in the job.
5. Although any such personal injury claim would be covered by the employer's public liability insurance, having such a claim will affect premiums, and may be a breach of insurance policies, which require employers to take reasonable steps to prevent employees being injured. In an extreme case, an insurer could decline cover.

Question

Ben has worked for you for nine months. Ben suffers from celiac disease, which means that he suffers an intolerance to wheat. Your offices are next to a factory that processes wheat for the product it produces. The factory produces a great deal of dust that is emitted into the air in and around the building.

Ben has taken time off on sick leave because of the effects of the dust on his health. Ben has been suffering from extreme stomach cramps and other symptoms. You have received a letter from Ben's doctor informing you that the reason for the aggravated symptoms is the dust in the air from the factory next door.

What are Ben's rights and what should you do?

Solution

Depending upon the severity and duration of Ben's condition (in particular its effect on his ability to carry out day-to-day activities), it is possible that celiac disease could amount to a 'disability' within the meaning of the Disability Discrimination Act. If this is the case then the company would be under an obligation, first, not to subject Ben to any detriment on the grounds of his disability and, second, to consider what reasonable adjustments can be made to his workplace or duties with a view to overcoming the effects of the disability.

These reasonable adjustments could include: seeking to reduce the emissions from the next-door factory by making enquiries to ascertain whether the factory is within the recommended guidelines for dust by-products, installing air conditioning in your office building or perhaps just in Ben's office, moving Ben to an office further away from the factory or allowing Ben to carry out his duties from home.

If none of these adjustments is possible or practicable or would not have the effect of overcoming the illness then it may be necessary to consider terminating the employment. The company is, of course, under a positive duty to protect the health and safety of its employees, and if it believes that an employee's health is being adversely affected by the working environment and there is nothing that can be done to prevent that, then it may be in both the company's and, ultimately, the employee's best interests to be removed from that environment.

Question

Mary works as a typist within a pool of secretaries for a firm of insurance brokers. The company has a policy that as soon as an employee has had five days' absence within two months, a disciplinary warning is given to the employee in an attempt to manage absence.

Mary developed clinical depression which caused her to have a number of days off and she triggered the disciplinary policy a number of times until, after she was given several written warnings and a chance to improve her attendance rate, she was dismissed.

Would Mary have a discrimination claim?

Solution

Mary may be able to bring a claim under the Disability Discrimination Act 1995. Mary then has to show that her clinical depression is a disability that falls under the Act. Since December 2005, it is no longer necessary for someone with a mental impairment to show that it is also a 'clinically well-recognized condition'. Mary does need to show that the depression is having a substantial and long-term adverse impact on her ability to carry out day-to-day activities. This would be gauged by considering a diagnosis by her doctor, and it may be that her employer has sought medical advice from its own company doctor, if it has one, who may also have an opinion on this. However, these ultimately are legal and not medical questions; so the Tribunal is guided by medical reports, but use their own judgement. As the disability must be long term, the depression must have lasted or is likely to last for 12 months.

If Mary is able to meet the definition of disability, the insurance brokers will attempt to show that the detrimental treatment, ie the dismissal, was justified. In doing so, an Employment Tribunal will look at how the company dealt with Mary, and if the company made no attempt to look into the causes of the disability to see whether it could make any reasonable adjustments, it is unlikely that it will be able to justify its actions. If the company had dismissed her on a general assumption that employees with depression cannot be relied upon, this would not be a reason that is 'material' because it does not relate to Mary's particular circumstances. Further, if her absence record was only slightly worse than other employees, it would probably not be regarded as substantial enough to justify her dismissal. The Tribunal will also want to know whether the company really needed Mary at work in order to justify her dismissal, or whether the other typists within the pool could easily have dealt with the workload during her absences.

The duty to make reasonable adjustments would include considering whether, owing to her disability, Mary would have appreciated working part-time hours which would have aided perhaps a return to work on full-time hours at a later stage.

Mary could also have a claim for unfair dismissal on the basis that a fair procedure was not followed if, for example, the company did not seek her own thoughts on her absences, and whether the employer really needed to dismiss her at all. The company must also take care to ensure that it has followed the statutory Disciplinary and Dismissal Procedures, in force from 1 October 2004.

? Question

Jean Jones applied for the position of administrator at a university near where she lived. She suffered from mild dyslexia which resulted in her being slow at the work she was required to undertake. She was not asked at the interview whether she had any difficulties that might affect the way in which she would carry out the work and she did not volunteer the information.

The university appointed her, but it soon became clear that she was getting behind with the job owing to her condition. The university discovered the truth.

Is it entitled to dismiss her on the grounds that, owing to mild dyslexia, Jean is incapable of completing all the tasks her predecessor could complete in the course of each day and would need an assistant to be able to cope?

Solution !

Jean, an administrator, is dyslexic and did not volunteer this information at her interview.

At interview, employers should only ask about a disability if it is, or may be, relevant to the person's ability to do the job. If the response is positive, such that the applicant has a disability, that should not be an automatic bar to the job. Instead the employer should assess whether the applicant is still suitable having considered reasonable adjustments. The employer should avoid asking discriminatory questions of one applicant that are irrelevant and that are not asked of all applicants.

Jean will, in all probability, be able to show that her dyslexia is a mental impairment which has a substantial and long-term adverse effect on her ability to carry out normal day-to-day activities, such as memory, or ability to concentrate, and that were she to be dismissed, this would be for a reason relating to her disability. She will therefore have a disability discrimination claim. The university will then have to justify the discrimination.

First, is the reason to dismiss material and substantial? The university will have to prove that her condition was affecting her productivity to such an extent that it was substantial as compared to the output of other employees and that because she was an administrator, the need for her to be able to read and write correctly at speed was material to her job.

As for reasonable adjustments, it could be unreasonable to expect the university to recruit an assistant, taking into account the financial and other costs that would be involved and the university's financial resources. The university should, as a matter of course, check to see if any financial assistance is available to help with such recruitment. It will also be expected to have considered other alternatives, such as allocating some of the work to another person or transferring Jean to another job.

The fact that Jean did not tell the university that she had a disability is immaterial, as she was not directly asked if she would have any difficulties that might affect the way she carried out the work. Had she been asked and had she responded in the negative, the university would be in a position to consider disciplinary action against her for the untruth but it would still have to deal with the disability as above.

DISCRIMINATION – AGE

? Question

You currently offer medicals to employees over the age of 50, but do not offer medicals to anyone below that age. It has been suggested that this will no longer be allowed under the Age Discrimination

Regulations. What can you do? Will you have to offer the medicals to everyone?

Solution

A policy of giving medicals to certain employees based on their age is now directly discriminatory under the Employment Equality (Age) Regulations 2006, which were introduced in October 2006. Presumably, you have decided to limit these medicals and tests to your older employees on the basis that you feel they are the ones more likely to need them, and that it would be unduly expensive to offer them to all employees.

You could argue that the employees in this scenario are not being treated **less favourably** but rather that they are being treated **differently** and that they are being treated differently on the basis of solid medical evidence. It would be a good idea to gather some evidence now – possibly through your occupational health specialist if you have one – to back up your presumption that employees over the age of 50 are more likely to become ill and therefore will benefit more from medical health checks.

There are two scenarios in which an employee could conceivably bring an age-related claim arising from this policy: 1. An older employee fails a medical and, as a result, his employment is terminated or his role is changed in a way that he regards as detrimental. He might claim that a younger employee would never have been given such a medical and his employment would not have been terminated or his role changed as a result. 2. A younger employee becomes ill and brings a claim that, had he been older, his illness would have been spotted earlier. Unless you can objectively justify your policy of limiting medicals and tests to older employees then it will amount to direct age discrimination.

It is difficult to tell at this stage what approach the Tribunals will take to the question of objective justification. The Regulations say that in order to justify an act of age discrimination, you must be pursuing a 'legitimate aim' – for example, encouraging loyalty, rewarding experience, or maintaining health and safety – and the means of pursuing this aim must be 'proportionate'. This means that the business benefit must be sufficient to outweigh the discriminatory effect, and that if there are two ways of achieving a similar business aim the least discriminatory way must be chosen.

In the first sort of claim above, you would have a strong argument for saying that your 'legitimate aim' in testing your older employees' health and making adjustments to their roles if necessary was 'protecting the health and safety of employees'. You would have a strong argument that the potential harm outweighed the discriminatory effect in this case and that the measure was also proportionate and therefore justified.

The second sort of claim above is more likely to be brought as a personal injury claim and would therefore be handled by your insurers. However, in the unlikely event that an employee did bring an age discrimination claim against you in a Tribunal, you would again have to show that the policy of not offering medicals and health tests to younger employees was objectively justified.

The Age Regulations make it clear that expense alone is not a 'legitimate aim' and therefore an argument that offering these medicals and tests to everyone was unduly expensive is unlikely to succeed. It would be worth getting some information about how much it would cost you to offer these medicals and tests to all of your employees regardless of their age. Without a doubt, the best practice would be to extend the tests and medicals to all employees and therefore avoid the risk of age discrimination claims altogether.

However, even if you decide not to extend the policy to all employees regardless of age, the fact that you have checked out the cost of doing so may provide you with some justification defence. The way you could argue this is:

- We have decided it is prohibitively expensive to offer these tests and medicals to all of our employees.
- If we were forced to treat all employees the same regardless of age, we would have to withdraw the medicals from everybody.
- We don't want to do this as we feel, based on the medical evidence (see above), that they are useful in safeguarding employees' health and safety.
- Therefore, we have decided the practice is justified.

While there is no guarantee of this defence succeeding, it does at least have more chance of succeeding than the alternative argument of 'it's too expensive so we're not doing it'.

In conclusion, then, if you decide you are not going to extend these medicals to all employees in the light of the new Age Regulations, you should gather evidence now on how much it would cost to do so and medical evidence to back up your presumption that older people are more likely to need the medicals you are offering them. These two pieces of evidence together will give you the best possible chance of defending any future age discrimination claim.

Question

Bert is 63 and a senior manager. He regularly makes jokes about his 'poor memory' and says it is because he is 'past it'. A younger member of the management team has made the same comment to Bert, as a joke, but Bert has taken offence.

Is Bert likely to be successful in his harassment claim?

Solution

The Employment Equality (Age) Regulations 2006 have introduced the concept of age-related harassment into UK employment law. For an employee or worker to prove harassment, they will need to show that, **on the grounds of age**, they have been subjected to **unwanted conduct** which has the purpose or effect of: (i) violating their dignity; or (ii) creating an intimidating, hostile, degrading, humiliating or offensive environment. Employers are vicariously liable for the actions of their employees unless they have taken reasonable steps to prevent the behaviour of that employee.

Quite what will be regarded as age-related harassment is unclear and will doubtless be the subject of a number of Tribunal claims in the coming years. The Department of Trade and Industry's consultation document on the subject of age-related harassment suggests that situations where 'a person makes light-hearted jokes about his own age and another person repeats the comment to him in the same context' will not constitute harassment.

This suggests that Bert's claim would not succeed. However, it is advisable that employers train their employees about the Age Regulations and, in particular, the fact that age-related jokes, which might previously have been seen as harmless fun, can now lead to Tribunal claims in exactly the same way as jokes about the colour of people's skin or their sexuality.

Question

Bert's young son Jim works for the same organization. One of his colleagues has made jokes about him 'bringing his old fogey of a dad to work' and asked whether they share an invalid car... Jim has taken offence.

Is Jim's harassment claim likely to succeed?

Solution

As above, for an employee or worker to prove harassment under the Employment Equality (Age) Regulations 2006, they will need to show that, **on the grounds of age**, they have been subjected to **unwanted conduct** which has the purpose or effect of: (i) violating their dignity; or (ii) creating an intimidating, hostile, degrading, humiliating or offensive environment.

The phrase 'on grounds of age' is wider than 'on grounds of **that particular person's age**' and could include, for example, a person taking offence on behalf of another person. Therefore, even though the jokes are not directed at Jim, he could still bring a harassment claim for jokes made about his father which he has found offensive on the grounds of age.

Question

One of your employees is approaching his 65th birthday. He has already suggested he would like to stay on after retirement. Unknown to him, you are planning to close his department and make everyone redundant. You would quite like him to stay on for a short time after his retirement – to help with the close down – but you will want to retire him after a few months.

Can you achieve this? How will the Age Discrimination Regulations affect this situation?

Solution

You can certainly agree to keep this employee on after his 65th birthday. The Age Discrimination Regulations came into force on 1 October 2006 and they are very much aimed at encouraging employers to keep their employees on after 65.

Since October 2006, employees over the age of 65 have been able to claim unfair dismissal and are also entitled to receive redundancy payments if their employment is terminated by reason of redundancy (previously, employees have lost these entitlements as soon as they hit the Normal Retirement Age).

The Regulations contain a (fairly) simple procedure for 'retiring' employees once they have reached the age of 65. If handled correctly, you could 'retire' this person at any stage without the risk of an unfair dismissal claim and without the need to pay any statutory redundancy.

The procedure (which you will have to follow for all your employees when you want them to retire) involves you writing to the employee at least six months before you want him to retire, informing him of the date on which you want him to retire and telling him that he has the right (if he wishes) to request staying on working longer. If he does make such a request, you will have to arrange a meeting with him to discuss his request (at which he has the right to be accompanied), write to him after the meeting confirming your decision to retire him (assuming he has not managed to change your mind) and offer him the right of appeal. If he does appeal, you will have to arrange another meeting, at which again he will have the right to be accompanied.

This is all a very long-winded procedure – particularly given the fact that you will not actually have to give any reasons for your refusal – but the advantage to you of following this procedure is that the termination will be classed as a 'retirement' dismissal and the employee cannot claim that the dismissal was unfair or that he should be entitled to receive a redundancy payment.

You could simply allow this employment to carry on after his 65th birthday – as the Regulations allow you to 'retire' employees any time once they are over their Normal Retirement Age (65 in this case) by following the retirement procedures. If you do that, you will need to serve him with six months' notice of your intention to retire him when you do decide to do so, tell him he has the right to request to work longer and, if he does make such a request, follow through a series of meetings. At the end of that series of meetings, you will be able to turn down the request and the dismissal will be deemed 'fair' by reason of retirement.

However, another alternative – if you know roughly when you are going to be closing down his department – would be to write to him *now* telling him that you intend to retire him in six months' time, so giving him a new 'intended date of retirement' and offering him the right to request working longer. If you follow through the proper procedure, you will then be able to 'retire' him fairly on the new intended date of retirement. If he does make a request to work on after that new intended date of retirement, you can either refuse the request or – if you still require his services – set a new date for him to retire. If that new date is less than six months after the original retirement date, you will be able to terminate his employment by reason of 'retirement' on that date without having to go through the retirement procedures again. If the new date is more than six months after the original retirement date – or if you allow the new retirement date to pass without dismissing him on that date – you will have to serve another six months' notice of another new intended date of retirement and follow through the retirement procedures again before you can dismiss fairly on the grounds of 'retirement'.

So, there is some scope for terminating this employee's employment after he has passed his 65th birthday without having to pay him a redundancy payment – provided you are able to be very organized over dates. If you want complete freedom to terminate his employment on any date, you may have to accept you will be paying him a redundancy payment.

? Question

Frank is a loyal employee who has been working for your company for the last 17 years. He will be 65 in two months' time; you are planning his retirement and wanting to start recruiting a replacement as soon as possible.

Can you do this?

Solution !

Assuming Frank does not have more contractual notice, he is entitled to at least 12 weeks' statutory notice.

The Employment Equality (Age) Regulations 2006 ('the Age Regulations') came into force on 1 October 2006, requiring employers to give at least 6 (and up to 12) months' written notice of their intention to retire an employee.

You are therefore obliged to give Frank at least six months' notice of the intended retirement date, inform him of his right to request not to retire and that this entitlement to make such a request runs until three months before the intended retirement date. If you fail to give Frank at least six months' notice of the intended retirement, you can still give him notification of the retirement up to two weeks before the date. However, Frank can then make a claim for late notification, and will be entitled to an award of up to eight weeks' pay (currently capped at £310 per week). Frank's deadline for making a request to stay on is extended to the retirement date, and his employment will continue until the process is completed. If you fail to notify Frank up to the date of dismissal, Frank may have a claim in the Employment Tribunal for late notification or unfair dismissal after he is dismissed.

If you fail to give Frank the six months' notice, but give him at least two weeks' notice, then Frank can make a claim for unfair dismissal: the reason for dismissal is not automatically deemed to be retirement. However, if you miss the two-week deadline, or fail to follow the procedure, then the dismissal is automatically unfair, and is also likely to be unlawful age discrimination.

If the Tribunal finds (as it almost certainly would) that the reason for dismissal was retirement, Frank's dismissal would be automatically unfair and he would be able to recover a Basic Award, loss of earnings and injury to feelings. The Age Regulations allow Frank to claim unfair dismissal after his 65th birthday – a major change in the law.

If Frank requests not to retire, you will be under a duty to consider the request before Frank is retired. You must hold a meeting (with a right to be accompanied by a fellow worker, but not a union representative) to consider the request and then inform Frank of your decision in writing afterwards. You do not have to give Frank a reason for refusal but cannot dismiss him until the day after the decision is communicated to him, which must be as soon as reasonably practicable.

Following your decision, Frank will have a right to an appeal meeting to reconsider your decision to retire him. Once again, you are not required to give reasons if you uphold the decision.

Assuming that you have given Frank at least six months' notice of retirement, if Frank is late in requesting not to retire (his request is less than three months before the notified intended retirement date) or does not make a request at all, you are under no duty to consider a request and can go ahead with his retirement dismissal on the intended retirement date.

You are not under a duty to consider Frank's request to continue working in good faith, so there is no reason in law why you should not start making preparations for his anticipated retirement by advertising or appointing his replacement. The right to request is just that, 'request', and refusal does not require explanation. However, you should remember that it is possible for employees to challenge your decision to retire them on other grounds of discrimination, such as sex, race or disability. ACAS guidelines suggest that as a matter of good practice, employers should give reasons, and also ensure that they develop a consistent approach to refusing or accepting requests to work beyond retirement age.

See also page 41.

DISCRIMINATION – AGE AND SEXUAL ORIENTATION

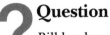 **Question**

Bill has been unsuccessful in a job interview. Feedback from the employer states that part of the reason for his being unsuccessful is that he 'would not fit in well with the existing team.' Bill is aged 59 and gay. He brings a claim for age and sexual orientation discrimination. Where does the employer stand?

Solution

In most discrimination claims there will not be evidence of outright acts of discrimination. In recognition of this, a finding of discrimination can be made on the basis of inference. Both the Employment Equality (Sexual Orientation) Regulations 2003 and the Employment Equality (Age) Regulations 2006 (as well as all other anti-discrimination legislation) contain provisions dealing with the burden of proof. The effect is that if a Tribunal finds that there is no other logical reason for the employer's actions, it can infer that the employer acted that way for discriminatory reasons. It is therefore important to ensure that there are clear, objective, measurable and non-discriminatory reasons for decisions such as failure to recruit. 'Not fitting in well with a team' is a very loose concept, and in many instances something of a smokescreen for what are in fact discriminatory reasons. Use of language like this should be avoided.

Chapter 2

Contracts of employment

? Question

Betty is a receptionist at your company. Last week Betty went on holiday and as far as you were concerned she was heading off for a couple of weeks in the sun.

However, you have just received a telephone call from Betty's husband and he has advised you that Betty has in fact had a nose-job. Unfortunately the operation didn't go quite to plan and Betty will not be able to return to work next week as expected. Betty's husband has also asked if Betty can cancel the rest of her holiday and be paid sick pay instead.

Do you have to cancel Betty's holiday and consider it to be sick leave instead? Do you have to pay Betty sick pay?

Solution !

Betty has requested sick leave following an elective cosmetic surgery procedure. You normally pay for genuine sickness absence, so how will you approach this situation where the problem is self-induced?

Start by looking at your contracts and policies – if Betty's contract or the relevant sick leave policy states that employees are entitled to sick pay in any situation where the employee is covered by a medical certificate with no restrictions, then you will be obliged to pay Betty sick pay.

Contracts should also deal with what happens if an employee falls sick on holiday. In the absence of a specific clause to the contrary, there is no obligation on an employer to 'cancel' a period of holiday and to treat it as sick leave.

Going on to consider the period after the holiday, ie if Betty does not return to work after the holiday and claims she is 'sick', if your sick pay policy states that entitlement to sick leave and pay is at the discretion of the company you will be able to withhold sick pay in this situation, and you can advise Betty that she will be on unpaid leave.

In future, if your sickness policy is not clear, set exclusions on when employees such as Betty will be entitled to receive sick pay and take sick leave, even if medical certificates cover them. Ensure that any entitlement is always at the discretion of the company and that self-inflicted injuries in particular are excluded.

Decide on a maximum number of days' sick leave that will be paid by the company each year, and stick to it. You could also set a qualifying length of service on the sick policy, for example six or twelve months' service must be attained before employees are entitled to company sick pay.

Remember, ultimately you are not obliged to have a company sick pay scheme at all, you are only required to pay statutory sick pay, but if you are going to pay company sick pay ensure that you have the discretion to vary, amend or stop payments where you deem it appropriate. However, even where payment is said to be discretionary, you should ensure that you do not exercise that discretion in a perverse or irrational way.

? Question

Kate has been absent from work on sick leave, fully certified by her doctor. Kate's company sick pay is about to expire and she rings you to find out if she can return to work.

The company wants Kate to stay off work on sick leave until it is happy that she is well again. Will the company have to pay her full pay?

Solution **!**

Kate has been certified by her doctor as being unfit for work, therefore the company is entitled to treat her as being unfit for work until there is a certificate from a doctor saying otherwise.

This does not mean that the company cannot, if it so wishes, let Kate return to work without being certified fit by her doctor. Simply the lapse of the last sickness certificate can be enough, although the passage of time will not necessarily mean that Kate is fully recovered.

Kate was undeniably sick in the first place. Once having been sick, she remains sick until she produces satisfactory evidence that she is no longer sick. The desire to return to work is not satisfactory evidence that she is no longer sick.

In the Employment Appeal Tribunal (EAT) case of *Beveridge* v. *KLM UK Ltd* (2000), an employee had produced for her employer, after a long spell of being certified unfit for work, a certificate that she was now fit. The employer wanted to get confirmation of her fitness from its own doctor, but this took some time and the employee was not paid whilst that clearance was awaited. The EAT held that, in the absence of a specific contractual provision to the contrary, an employee who was 'proffering her services against a background of a certificate of good health' was entitled to be paid.

In summary, unless Kate has such a certificate of 'good health' the company does not have to allow her to return to work and does not have to pay her once her company sick pay has been exhausted.

With respect to long-term sickness absences, you should also bear in mind the Disability Discrimination Act 1995 (DDA), as the employee's illness may amount to a disability, which would mean that you need to consider whether you could make any reasonable adjustments to enable her to get back to work.

Question

The company retirement age is 60. Your boss wants an employee just about to have his 60th birthday to carry on working, but does not want him to have unfair dismissal or redundancy rights.

Can you do this?

Solution

No, you cannot. The law in this area changed significantly on 1 October 2006, when Regulations outlawing age discrimination in employment came into force. There is now a default retirement age of 65, but if your company wishes to keep an earlier retirement age, such as 60, this will need to be objectively justified, and in practice this is likely to be very difficult indeed. Other than in very exceptional cases, 65 should be regarded as the standard retirement age. So you should take the view that the existing retirement age as set out in the contract no longer stands.

Any attempt to dismiss this employee prior to his 65th birthday is likely to be an automatic unfair dismissal.

An employee can make a request to work beyond the age of 65 (or any earlier retirement age, if justified – see above). Meetings and discussions have to take place, and the employer can decline the request. Where the employer accepts an employee's request to continue working after the age of 65 (or an earlier normal retirement age, if that can be objectively justified), it will need to notify the employee of the new retirement date, and go through the procedural requirements again.

See also pages 30–38.

Question

An employee, widowed a year ago, has children aged 7, 9 and 11. In the last twelve months he has had 14 spells of absence, each of 1 or 2 days, for things such as 'tummy ache' or 'headache'. His manager says she believes that in every case the illness was actually that of one of the children.

Can his manager challenge him about this?

Solution

It looks here as if there may be abuse of a contractual sick pay scheme, but that will depend on a) whether the manager's suspicions are true and b) the terms of any such scheme. Statutory Sick Pay (SSP) rules make clear that the illness concerned must be that of the employee him/herself, not someone else, but such short absences would not normally qualify for SSP and not all contractual schemes are so explicit. From a contractual point of view there is also the question of whether, in the circumstances here, a term might be implied that taking time off for children's' sickness is OK: what, over the 12 months concerned and in the light of her suspicions, has the manager said to the employee?

It is not clear whether the absence has been paid or unpaid. Even if it has been unpaid, however, it may involve misconduct in the sense of unauthorized absence. Again, however, there may be no express rules on the topic and, even if there are, they would have to be interpreted in the light of the manager's reaction over the last twelve months. An employer's failure to enforce express rules in the past does not deprive it of the right to do so in the future, but it does mean that the employer would first have to make clear that it was intending to change its approach to their enforcement.

The circumstances here look as though the statutory right to 'time off for dependants' might apply. The relevant legislation provides that 'An employee is entitled to be permitted by his employer to take a reasonable amount of time off during the employee's working hours in order to take action which is necessary [...] to provide assistance on an occasion when a dependant falls ill [...or ...] to make arrangements for the provision of care for a dependant who is ill' and a child is a dependant for these purposes. It is, however, important to remember that:

a. this is a right to unpaid time off;
b. it is intended to cover emergencies, the making of arrangements for – rather than actually providing – longer-term care for sick dependants;
c. its exercise is dependent on the employee telling the employer that the time is being taken off for this purpose.

Probably the best approach in this case is to regard it as identifying a possible future problem, rather than actually being a past problem. The employee needs to be advised, as sympathetically as possible, what the 'rules' – both contractual and statutory – are and how the employer intends to apply them in the future. The manager needs to be told this, too.

See also Chapter 8.

Question

During a recent period of rather bad weather, several employees who live in fairly remote locations phoned to say they couldn't get to work owing to 'icy roads', 'fallen trees blocking access' or simply 'it's too cold for my car'. They said that they would do some 'paperwork' at home.

But if they can't get in, do you still have to pay them?

Solution

The short answer is probably 'no', unless the contract provides for payment in such circumstances. Generally, under the contract (whether expressly in writing or implied), you are only legally obliged to pay someone for what they are contracted to do, so, if they are not there to fulfil their contractual obligations, you do not have to pay them. This is the case even if it is not their fault, for example the weather has stopped them from being able to get into work. What's more, you do not need their consent, written or voiced, to deduct the appropriate sums from their pay. The Deductions from Wages provisions in Part II of ERA 1996, requiring previous written authorization or a contractual term, only apply where the employer fails to pay the wages properly due under the contract: here, as the employee has failed to perform their contractual obligation to perform work, the employer is simply paying the correct contractual wages.

You should also see what has happened in the past in similar circumstances. If previously employees have been paid in these circumstances, they may be able to argue that this has become an implied contractual term, via custom and practice. Even if this is not the case, you may need to give notice that this practice will change from now on.

However, you might, quite reasonably, decide to exercise your discretion and pay them anyway. Or you might suggest they take the time as paid annual leave. Be careful here though, if other members of staff become aware that they could be paid to stay at home, you might find a whole host of interesting excuses coming your way!

? Question

You employ a part-timer, Louise, who normally works just on a Tuesday and Thursday. Naturally Louise gets the same pro-rated holiday entitlement as your full-time employees (four weeks). However, because she is not at work on a Monday or Friday, she misses out on public holidays. Louise says she is entitled to be paid for them.

Will you have to pay Louise?

Solution

The short answer is maybe!

If, as is often the case, your full-time workers aren't required to work on public holidays and they have them off in addition to their annual leave entitlement, ie four weeks plus the eight public holidays, then it is arguable that your part-timers should get the same on a pro rata basis, ie subject to the point made below that their holiday entitlement should be pro-rated from 28 days rather than 20 days. This is because the Part Time Workers (Prevention of Less Favourable Treatment) Regulations require you to treat part-timers the same as full-timers. There is a defence to less favourable treatment – if you can justify it, probably on economic grounds. But in respect of holidays, it will be very difficult to show why full-timers should get more.

However, in *McMenemy* v. *Capita Business Services* (2006), the EAT held that part-timers who didn't work on Mondays were not entitled to a pro rata apportionment of extra time off. The reason that they didn't get the benefit was because they did not work on Mondays, not because they were part-timers. However, the case involved a business which operated on a seven days a week basis, and so full-timers (those working a five-day week) who didn't work on Mondays also did not get extra time off for those holidays. It may be that if your organization operates on a Monday to Friday basis, Louise may be entitled on a pro rata basis.

So, find out which public holidays the part-timers do not actually have access to (eg they may have access to Christmas Day and New Year's Day as this may fall on their working day) and then pro rata to them either the additional time off or pay in lieu of that additional time off that they should have in respect of the public holidays.

Note also that the government intends to add Bank holidays to the statutory entitlement to paid holiday under the Working Time Regulations ('Success at Work: Strategy Paper', 2006).

Question

Owing to operational needs a new shift pattern is to be introduced, and this will result in contracts of employment having to be changed. Most employees have accepted, but a few refuse to sign the new contracts and to work the new shifts.

Can you impose the contractual changes? Can you dismiss those who refuse to sign?

Solution

In the absence of an express contractual entitlement allowing the employer to vary working hours/shift patterns or, at the very least, a long-standing 'custom and practice' of regular changes to working hours, an employer does not have the right to change this contractual term unilaterally. Although this is sometimes overlooked, a contract of employment is governed by the same principles that apply to the contracts between the company and, say, its suppliers and customers, and once a contract has been entered into, one party cannot simply change the terms to suit itself.

Therefore, if the company seeks to impose this contractual change without consent it will be placing itself in breach of contract and, most importantly in the employment context, this will give the employees the right to resign and claim constructive unfair dismissal. Alternatively, if the changes have an impact on wages, the employees may continue working 'under protest', and use the Deductions from Wages provisions in Part II of ERA 1996 to claim the difference between the wages they receive and the wages properly due under the (old) contract.

The employer would therefore be better advised to terminate the contracts of those who refuse to sign up to the new arrangements, giving proper contractual notice, and offering re-engagement with immediate effect, on the new terms and conditions. Although such a strategy still runs the risk that the dismissals are unfair, the company would defend any claims on two grounds:

i.   'Some other substantial reason' – this potentially fair reason is used if the company can show that there were good business reasons for this change. If challenged, the Tribunal would look at the business needs for the changes, the method used before implementing the changes and the reasonableness of the employees' decision to refuse the changes.

In establishing that there is a sound business reason, the company will not have to show that the business was on the verge of financial collapse, but just that the changes were necessary for the better running of the business.

Procedure is also important here. The Tribunal will look at the way that the company implemented the changes, and whether it consulted adequately with the employees about the reasons that the changes were necessary. Note that it will be necessary to comply with the statutory disciplinary and dismissal procedures.

ii. Redundancy – this would be on the basis that the company's need for employees to work particular shifts had ceased and that the company had offered 'suitable alternative employment', ie the new shift arrangements. This, however, is something of a fallback position in this situation; some other substantial reason is the main approach.

It should also be noted that even if the defence fails and there is a finding of unfair dismissal, by offering alternative employment the company should be able to limit compensation, as the dismissed employees are under a duty to mitigate their loss, and are likely to have failed to have done so by refusing the alternative.

Question

You ask a new employee to sign the company's standard contract, which contains a confidentiality clause. The employee refuses to sign it on the basis that it is in breach of his human right, freedom of expression.

What do you do?

Solution

Insist that the employee signs the contract!

First, the Human Rights Act 1998 (HRA) (which is the legislation incorporating the European Convention on Human Rights (ECHR) into UK law) applies only to public authorities or 'emanations of the state'. Therefore, if you are a private employer you could simply say that you are not covered by the HRA. However, courts and tribunals are under an obligation to interpret all laws in accordance with the principles of the HRA, which may be useful to the employee, although, in our view, it is unlikely to give them the right to bring direct action against a private employer simply on the basis of the HRA. But if employees have other claims against you, such as breach of contract, or unfair dismissal, the courts and tribunals will consider their Convention rights, such as their Article 10 right to freedom of expression.

Even if you are found to be a public authority or 'emanation of the state', the right to freedom of expression contained in Article 10 of the HRA is by no means unfettered. The exceptions are contained in Article 10 (2): 'The exercise of these freedoms, since it carries with it duties and responsibilities, may be subject to such formalities, conditions, restrictions or penalties as are prescribed by law and are necessary in a democratic society... for preventing the disclosure of information received in confidence...'.

The ECHR also protects the right to privacy (Article 8), and this will be balanced against any claim concerning Article 10. The HRA is also interpreted using the principle of 'proportionality'. Therefore, provided the proposed restriction is 'proportionate' to your legitimate interest in the commercial confidentiality that it is seeking to protect, it is highly unlikely to be a breach of human rights.

Question

An employee is being investigated for theft at work, and at a meeting with his manager he denies the allegations. The next day he phones in sick and you receive a doctor's certificate signing him off with 'stress'. He then refuses to see Occupational Health 'on doctor's orders' and refuses to take any further part in the investigation or disciplinary.

What should you do?

Solution

If the employee has been signed off for a relatively short time then the first step may be simply to wait until the certificate has expired and then recommence the procedure when the employee is able to return to work. As the employee is off the premises there is no immediate need to terminate employment in the interests of security. The employee's entitlement to sick pay during this period will depend on the company's policy, and on the individual's contract of employment.

If the period of certification continues for an unreasonable period and the employee refuses to attend the company's occupational health adviser then the company should seek the employee's consent for it to obtain a medical report from his GP. If the consent is given and if the medical report suggests that the employee will be fit within a 'reasonable' period then, again, the company should wait until that period has expired and the employee is fit before recommencing the procedure.

If the employee withholds consent for his GP to prepare a report then this may be a breach of contract on his part provided the company has an appropriate clause in its handbook or contracts. If the employee continues to refuse to cooperate then the company could conclude the investigation and dismiss him in his absence. However, this should only be done after the company has taken all reasonable steps to get the employee to cooperate, given him the opportunity to make representations at any hearing either in person, in writing or by a representative, and warned him expressly of the likely consequences of failing to cooperate.

Question

Denise used to live within easy reach of her workplace; however, following a merger between her employer and a larger rival, Denise's workplace relocated and is now nearly five hours away. Denise was a valued member of staff, so her contract was enhanced by adding a company car, as well as giving her an accommodation allowance, enabling her to stay in digs during the working week.

Unfortunately, Denise has been signed off sick for six months as she is suffering from carpel tunnel syndrome, rendering her unable to drive. Her company car is actually needed by another member of staff.

Can you get it back, and do you continue to pay Denise's accommodation allowance whilst she is at home?

Solution

The answer to this question is dependent mainly on what Denise's contract of employment states, or whether there is any other document which contains provisions relating to the accommodation allowance and the company car. If Denise's contract states that during any period of illness the company is entitled to request that the company car be returned, or that the accommodation allowance will not be paid to Denise, then the matter is straightforward and the employer will not need any extra authority apart from that within the contract to take this action. Even where it is not in the contract, there may be provisions within, for example, a company car policy and again, as long as Denise was aware of the policy and the employer exercises the policy in a reasonable manner, this should be a straightforward situation.

Where the employer does not have contractual authority to take the action that it wishes to, and there is no relevant policy, the two issues would probably be best dealt with separately. The reason that the company car needs to be returned is because another employee needs to use it. So it may be possible to negotiate with Denise and ask her whether she would return the car and in the circumstances she would be paid a car allowance for the loss of the benefit.

With regard to the accommodation allowance, it is less likely that Denise would have any discussions with you as she would be losing remuneration, and in these circumstances it would be difficult to establish a sound business reason for trying to vary her contract to allow you to withdraw the accommodation allowance, as it is simply to save the employer money. Unless there are severe financial circumstances affecting the employer, which may have created a business necessity to stop the accommodation allowance, it is unlikely that you will be able to withdraw this without her permission to do so. This is why it is important to make it clear in the contract that the accommodation allowance is payable only in respect of the actual use of accommodation. Otherwise, Denise may be able to bring an action for unlawful deduction of wages.

As this Headache demonstrates, it is advisable to draft documents in such a way as to give the employer maximum flexibility. Specifically with regard to company cars, the contract should state that you are entitled to collect the company car where the employee is on a long-term absence (say for three weeks or more) and to specify whether in those circumstances the employee is entitled to an allowance for loss of the company car, or whether he or she is not entitled to any compensation during the period that the company car is returned to the company.

Question

Rebecca is a fitness instructor at a leisure centre, and has been there for three years. Rebecca has just been made Employee of the Month, after which she overheard one of her male colleagues insisting to another that 'she is so butch she is either a lesbian or on steroids'.

Rebecca complains to the HR manager at the leisure centre who tells her that there is no action that she can take. Rebecca is not very happy, and in any event a friend of hers has become manager of a competing leisure centre and has offered Rebecca a job there. Rebecca resigns and claims constructive dismissal.

What are her chances of succeeding?

Solution

To succeed in constructive dismissal, Rebecca will need to show that her employer committed a fundamental breach of contract; that she resigned because of that breach, and that she did not waive the breach.

There is also a potential claim here for sex discrimination, and discrimination on grounds of sexual orientation. The remarks may be viewed as sexual harassment under the Sex Discrimination Act 1975 (SDA), as it is arguable that referring to someone as a lesbian is sexual conduct, which violates her dignity, or creates an intimidating etc environment. The remarks may also amount to sexuality discrimination, regardless of whether Rebecca is a lesbian or not, as less favourable treatment on grounds of perceived sexuality is unlawful under the Employment Equality (Sexual Orientation) Regulations 2003.

The employer is vicariously liable for the harassing behaviour of other employees, unless it can show that it took such steps as were reasonably practical to prevent the behaviour. When an allegation like this emerges, an employer should investigate by speaking with the other employees involved to find out their side of the story. If there is a case to answer, the employer should undertake a disciplinary hearing.

Rebecca would have a good argument that the employer's failure in this regard amounted to a fundamental breach of contract, entitling her to resign, especially as allegations of steroid taking could affect her reputation as a fitness instructor. However, following the introduction of the statutory Disciplinary and Dismissal Procedures (DDP) in October 2004, Rebecca will need to raise a grievance in writing first before pursuing a claim at Tribunal. If she does raise her complaint in writing, the failure by the employer to deal with this in accordance with the statutory procedures will mean that any compensatory award will be increased by between 10 and 50 per cent.

Did Rebecca resign as a result of the breach of contract? This would be a question of fact for the Employment Tribunal to decide and would depend on what evidence was put forward with regard to Rebecca's alternative job offer at another leisure centre. However, Tribunals have accepted that employees will often wait to find another job before resigning: as long as the employer's breach of contract is the effective cause of the resignation, the employee can claim for constructive dismissal.

Did Rebecca waive the breach of contract? A Tribunal will generally decide this point depending on the delay incurred by Rebecca in resigning after her employer had failed to take action and her attitude to that. If she complained to the HR manager, but did not resign until a few months afterwards and did not raise the complaint again, then a Tribunal may find that she waived that breach of contract.

Rebecca seems to have a reasonably good chance of succeeding.

? Question

A publishing house moves its offices from London to Southampton. The manager responsible for the London office tells the board of directors that he is unsure about going to the Southampton office, but enters into negotiations regarding compensation for added travelling costs, time and inconvenience. No agreement was reached and the manager resigned claiming constructive dismissal.

Would he have a successful claim?

Solution !

Before the manager can bring a claim for constructive dismissal, he must have one year's continuous service. If this is the case, then he must show that the employer has committed a fundamental breach of contract. He will also need to have followed the statutory grievance procedures, by putting his complaint in writing, before the Tribunal will admit the claim.

In doing so, the manager will need to show that the London office was his place of work and that there was no mobility clause in his contract requiring him to move or travel the additional miles to the new Southampton office. Even if there were such a mobility clause, it would have to cover these circumstances. For example, does the mobility clause expressly state that a move to a new office can be required on a permanent basis? Or that it will only permit a move to another office within a 'reasonable distance'? If so, is a move from London to Southampton reasonable? It may be important to show that the board of directors were aware that he did not want to move and that by entering into negotiations with him regarding compensation for added travelling time etc, they were accepting his position, and then by not accepting his reasonable demands, the employer committed a breach of contract.

Even where there is a mobility clause giving the employer the right to move an employee to another workplace, although there is no obligation to operate this in a reasonable manner, there is an obligation on the employer to act in a way that will not undermine the implied term of mutual trust and confidence. In *United Bank Ltd* v. *Akhtar* (1989) there was a mobility clause in the contract where an employee was transferred from Leeds to Birmingham, but the way it was dealt with was considered to amount to a fundamental breach of three implied terms. These were:

- that the employers would give reasonable notice of any transfer (in this case the employers gave very short notice of the transfer);
- that the employers would not exercise discretion to provide relocation expenses unfairly (in this case the employers did not provide such expenses);
- that the employers would not act in such a way as to undermine the mutual trust and confidence of the employment relationship.

However, the application of any implied terms will vary according to the circumstances of the particular case. So where an employee was given very short notice of moving to another site, it was not a fundamental breach of contract, even though the employers had taken a 'fairly cavalier attitude'. The employee was not required to move house and the move did not therefore affect him to any great extent (*Hart Builders (Edinburgh) Ltd* v. *Lyall*) (1992).

The manager would also have to show that he has resigned because of the breach of contract that he is complaining of, and that he has not waived the breach. So, for example, if he had moved down to the Southampton office and had continued to work there for a number of months whilst trying to negotiate new terms, a Tribunal may find that he had accepted the change in his contract of the place of work.

In general terms a unilateral change to a workplace without contractual authority to do so would usually amount to a fundamental breach of contract. In addition, the manager could claim that his position was redundant, as there is closure of his workplace. The way in which the matter was handled, ie not offering a redundancy option, may render this an unfair dismissal.

❓ Question

Heather is a successful agent for Abbey Health Products, a company that sells magnets with healing properties to pharmacies and similar businesses. Over the years she has built up a substantial network of contacts, and generates a great deal of business. Abbey has, however, never got round to asking Heather to sign a contract containing restrictive covenants. In fact she has no real contract at all, just a two-page offer letter. Heather resigns, giving the required three months' notice, and it seems likely that she is going to set up her own magnet-selling business. Abbey is very anxious to limit as much as possible her use of the customer connection, and wants to impose restrictive covenants regarding this. It also wants Heather to be on garden leave for the three-month notice period, and for the restrictive covenants to apply at the end of that garden leave period.

Can Abbey achieve these things?

Solution !

The general rule is that an employee can only be put on to garden leave if there is an express term in the contract. To try to force Heather on to garden leave without such a clause is therefore likely to be a breach of contract. Given the fact, however, that Heather has already resigned, this breach of contract does not have any particular financial consequences; Heather is entitled to three months in lieu of notice in any event, and the breach of contract simply brings the due date for payment of that amount forward. Of more significance, however, is the practical effect that Heather can ignore the instruction to go on to garden leave and treat herself as discharged from the contract of employment immediately, by reason of the employer's breach.

Had there been restrictive covenants in the contract, but no garden leave clause, the company's attempt, in breach of contract, to force Heather on to garden leave would have had other consequences. Where one party is in breach of contract, it cannot then rely on other terms of that contract. Thus, the restrictive covenants would be rendered unenforceable by Abbey if it had breached Heather's employment contract in this way.

It is always possible for the company to ask Heather to sign new restrictive covenants, but she of course has absolutely no incentive to do so. Abbey will therefore have to consider additional payments, over and above the three months in lieu of notice, to encourage Heather to enter into the covenants.

Since Heather had not signed a proper contract, we can assume that there is no payment in lieu of notice clause in the contract, but of course this needs to be checked. On the assumption that there is no such clause, the payment in lieu of notice can be paid tax-free up to £30,000. If there is going to be an additional payment for restrictive covenants, this needs to be separated out in any compromise agreement that is offered to her. Otherwise, the whole of the payment, including the tax-free element, becomes connected with the new restrictive covenants. HM Revenue and Customs is likely to take the position that, in the absence of any other analysis, the whole amount of the payment made to Heather was in return for her entering into new covenants. A payment in that context becomes taxable. Therefore, a separate amount, perhaps £1,000, should be allocated to the restrictive covenants and the balance of the payment up to £30,000 can be made tax-free.

Attempting to negotiate with Heather regarding restrictive covenants at this stage is bolting the door after the horse has gone, but if she declines, then there remains some level of action that Abbey can take. Customer lists and similar information remain the property of Abbey and need to be returned by Heather at the conclusion of her employment. This applies whether or not there are express confidentiality provisions in her contract of employment, as it would be covered by implied terms of confidentiality. Abbey is obviously in a much stronger position if Heather has signed the appropriate clauses.

If Heather sets up her own business and uses customer connections from her time at Abbey with which to launch that business, then it may be possible for Abbey, even in the absence of express restrictive covenants, to bring a case against her, on the basis of the 'springboard principle'. This arises where an ex-employee uses customer connections which rightfully belong to his or her ex-employer to launch a business. In some circumstances courts may be prepared to order an injunction preventing that use of an employer's confidential information, but these arguments are difficult to construct and an employer is in a much better position where there are express covenants.

Question

You have had a complaint from a group of senior employees that the board has acted unfairly and unreasonably by changing the way in which it adjusts their salaries. Rather than, as has previously happened with them and as is still happening with other groups of employees, giving the whole of the increase as an addition to basic salary, it has made only a small increase in basic salary but increased their 'car allowance' substantially. Although this means that their total remuneration is the same as it would otherwise have been, the 'car allowance' does not – as the basic salary would have done – count for pension purposes or when the annual bonus (which is given as a percentage of salary) is declared. You have some sympathy with their complaint.

What legal arguments might you be able to use to persuade the board to change its approach?

Solution

Although the complaint is of 'unfair' and 'unreasonable' treatment, there is no general rule of law that an employee must be treated 'fairly' or 'reasonably'. Where laws do require 'fair' treatment (eg in the context of unfair dismissal), they do so by defining – very precisely, and often in a way that does not coincide with any general usage of the word – what is 'fair'. And even though laws often do use the word 'reasonable' they:

- do so in specific contexts and any right of action relates to that context and not to the concept of 'reasonableness' itself;
- often include specific tests for what will, and what will not, for the stated purpose be regarded as 'reasonable' or 'unreasonable'; and
- require a balance to be struck between what looks 'reasonable' from two competing points of view. For instance, it will seldom be 'reasonable' from the employees' point of view for them to lose their job through no fault of their own: and yet redundancy is expressly recognized as a fair reason for dismissal and it is expressly recognized that it may be reasonable for an employer to rely on that reason in dismissing an employee.

One of the grounds for this complaint appears to be that the employees concerned are being treated differently from how other employees are being treated. The general rule so far as the law is concerned is that there is nothing wrong, with differences in treatment as such. What matter are the *reasons* for such differences. The list of prohibited reasons is long, and continues to grow: besides sex and race there are things like disability and part-time and fixed-term working and, since 1 October 2006, age. But if the reason for the difference of treatment does not appear on that list (or unless – see below – it involves a breach of the employee's contract) then the law does not prohibit it.

Another ground for this complaint appears to be that the employees concerned are being treated differently from how they have been treated in the past. It is quite common for employees to believe that 'if X has happened in the past, I am entitled to it in the future'. Sometimes, if what has happened in the past has happened with sufficient consistency and notoriety – 'everybody knows that X always happens' – it can acquire the status of an implied contractual term and so found a legal complaint if it ceases to happen. Are there, here, any grounds for arguing that it was a term (express or implied) in each employee's contract of employment that any increase in remuneration would always be given in any particular way? That would depend on information that the question does not give. But it would be unusual.

There is implied into every contract of employment a term that neither party will act in such a way as to breach the mutual trust and confidence on which the employment relationship is based. It has been held that for an employer arbitrarily or capriciously to treat one individual less favourably than all the rest of its employees – for example, by withholding a general pay increase – can breach that term. The essence of that breach, however, is that it is directed (without any reasonable justification) at the individual employee concerned. Here, that does not appear to be the case. It is a different group that is being treated differently – as a group, not as individuals.

It is also worth remembering in this context that if there is such a breach of the term of mutual trust and confidence by the employer then what the employee has to do is say that it so destroyed the fundamental basis of the relationship that he or she was going to treat the contract as at an end, and therefore has to resign and claim constructive dismissal. It is, of course, impossible to be sure that if any of the affected employees felt sufficiently aggrieved by what was going on they might resign and then make such a claim. But, first, giving up employment just for the chance of making such a claim is a pretty drastic step to take and, second, the chances of any such claim succeeding appear to be low because the employer's approach does not seem to be directed arbitrarily or capriciously at any individual: it deals with a group distinguished without any obvious reference (direct or indirect) to any of the forbidden discrimination categories.

You may wish to check that the arrangement is not resulting in any underpayment of tax but, even if it is, that will mean that the tax calculation is wrong, not that the approach itself is unlawful. You may also wish to check that the detailed rules of the relevant pension scheme are not being breached. It seems unlikely. Pension schemes normally refer to a pensionable salary but leave it up to the contract of employment to say what parts of the total remuneration package do, and do not, go into that pensionable salary.

In summary, despite the evident staff relations problems, the employer does not have too much legally to worry about here.

? Question

Your company's sales have recently been below par and you have decided to update your sales force contracts to include a more rigorous performance-related bonus scheme. You want to do this as soon as possible to improve performance and to avoid thinking about redundancies.

What do you do?

Solution !

The sort of change you are proposing appears to be a significant change to the contracts of employment as it may affect the earning potential of your sales force. Any significant change must be agreed with the employees before it can be adopted as a variation to the terms of employment. To do this you will need to consult with the sales force and seek their agreement to the change, citing the need for more sales and the avoidance of redundancies in future.

As long as the terms offered are sufficiently clear and targets seem achievable, it is unlikely that most of your sales force will resist the change. However, some may, and it is necessary to go through a reasonable consultation process before you can consider forcing through the change.

If it comes to the point that you need to take a hard line with some of the sales force, you cannot simply impose the changes. If you do, you are likely to face claims for unlawful deductions from wages, as the changes seem likely to affect pay. Also, employees could resign and make a claim for constructive unfair dismissal. Instead, you will need to terminate their old contracts, giving appropriate notice, and offer immediate re-engagement on the new contracts. You will need to consider terminating their contracts of employment and re-engaging them on the new terms, following the statutory procedures for dismissal (this assumes there are fewer than 20 employees involved).

As you have given them proper contractual notice, the employees cannot claim wrongful dismissal, as you have terminated their original contracts lawfully. You have dismissed them, so they can claim unfair dismissal, but you have dismissed them for a potentially fair reason, genuine business needs, which amounts to 'some other substantial reason'. The dismissals are unlikely to be unfair, as you have followed a fair procedure, by consulting them, and trying to seek agreement. By offering them alternative employment with similar earning potential, following a reasonable consultation period based on genuine business reasons and their contractual notice period before the new contract takes effect, they will be hard pressed to claim unfair dismissal as your reason for dismissal would have been for 'some other substantial reason' – a legitimate business need. Even if the Tribunal finds that the dismissals are unfair, because of some procedural failing, the amount of compensation awarded is likely to be small: even if they do claim successfully because the consultation or dismissal is flawed in some way, any claim would be likely to be very low because they would have failed to mitigate their loss by refusing the new contract and the income it would have provided. In such circumstances, compensation would be limited to the difference between their earnings under the old contract and what they could have earned under the new one.

CONTRACT/UNFAIR DISMISSAL

Question

Trevor is a salesman who has been with Media Marketing Limited for several years. His performance has always been suspect, and after a performance review process he is dismissed on grounds of capability. He brings an Employment Tribunal claim for unfair dismissal. He also claims that he is entitled to an additional bonus payment, and adds a breach of contract claim to his Employment Tribunal case.

Is this part of his claim valid?

When the company analyses its figures following Trevor's departure, it realizes that he had put through some suspect orders, which were incorrectly inflated, and which led to him being paid excess commission of about £20,000.

What action can the company now take?

Solution

Breach of contract claims can be brought in the Employment Tribunal by an employee up to a maximum of £25,000. Non-payment of a bonus, provided it was contractual, would come under this provision. Although Trevor could bring a County Court claim for his unpaid bonus, it makes sense for him to include this within the Tribunal claim.

The company is also able to bring a County Court action against Trevor for recovery of the £20,000, but in the circumstances there is a more convenient process. As well as defending the unfair dismissal, the employer is able to add a counterclaim. This can only be done, however, when the employee has first raised a contractual claim himself, and has thus triggered the Tribunal's contractual jurisdiction. If Trevor had pursued only a straightforward dismissal claim, without any mention of the alleged unpaid bonus, then the company would not have been able to lodge a counterclaim with the Employment Tribunal. Instead, the company would have had to bring separate proceedings in the County Court.

Such a counterclaim can be a useful deterrent in defending a Tribunal claim, and of course if it comes to settlement or assessment of any award, one may be set off against the other.

See also page 66.

Chapter 3

Transfers of Undertakings (Protection of Employment) Regulations (TUPE)

? Question

You are the facilities director of a company which has a number of offices and factories across the south of England. Your factories have on-site canteens and the management of these canteens is currently contracted out to Grub-at-Work Ltd.

The MD is dissatisfied with the management of Grub-at-Work Ltd as he thinks they are inefficient and are making too much profit out of the contract. He wants to do a number of things: terminate the contract with Grub-at-Work Ltd and bring the management of the canteens back 'in-house', get rid of the current catering manager and, finally, amend the contracts of the canteen staff so that they will be more 'mobile' between the various factories.

What issues does this give rise to?

Solution

1. What does the contract with Grub-at-Work say, if anything, about termination? Is there a notice period? Are there any provisions about what will happen to the staff on termination? Whilst it is not possible to contract out of the effects of TUPE (see below), the contract may contain restrictions on what Grub-at-Work can do to the staff in the period prior to termination (for example, not putting up their pay, moving them to other sites etc).

2. This is almost certain to fall within the TUPE Regulations 2006. TUPE provides that, where an undertaking is transferred, the contracts of employment of those employed in the undertaking immediately before the transfer go with it. The TUPE Regulations 2006 define a 'relevant transfer' as the 'transfer of an economic entity which retains its identity'. However, the government decided to add a new extended definition of a transfer where there is a 'service provision change'. This occurs whenever one person ceases to carry out service activities and another person carries those services out instead, and immediately before the change there was an organized grouping of employees with the principal purpose of carrying out those activities. This applies to a change of contractor, to contracting-out, and to contracting-in.

    This provision was introduced in order to bring greater certainty to service provision changes, by bringing almost all changes within the protection of the TUPE Regulations 2006. The only exceptions are where the services are in connection with a single specific event or task of short duration (such as organizing a conference), or where the activities consist wholly or mainly of the supply of goods for the client's use. The government decided to drop a proposed exception for 'professional services', such as legal or accountancy services.

    So it seems virtually certain that taking canteen management back 'in-house' will amount to a service provision change, even if it falls outside the general definition of a transfer.

    In determining whether or not there is an economic entity which retains its identity (the standard transfer definition), it is necessary to look at a number of factors, including:

    * whether or not any physical assets are transferring – in this case presumably this includes the canteen equipment;
    * whether there are any intangible assets transferring, such as goodwill, intellectual property rights – in this case probably not;
    * whether the employees are transferring – in this case the canteen staff other than the catering manager are required. It should be noted that one cannot prevent TUPE from applying by choosing not to take on the staff as the Tribunal will apply a purposive interpretation to TUPE and say that if TUPE should have applied but for your decision not to transfer the staff then, de facto, TUPE will apply and the staff should come across.

    Will the undertaking retain its identity? That is, will it perform largely the same functions for the same customers in much the same way?

This is a broad brush test and, we would suggest, a canteen service in the same premises for the same customers will retain its identity.

When TUPE applies, it has the following main consequences:

- There is an obligation to inform and consult with elected employee representatives about the transfer and its consequences. If there is no trade union in place then Grub-at-Work Ltd will need to ask the employees in the various canteens to elect representatives. They will then commence consultation and your company will be obliged to inform Grub-at-Work about any 'measures' you propose, which could include any redundancies or proposed changes to terms and conditions (although see below). The penalty for failure to consult is an award of up to 13 weeks' pay per employee. The TUPE Regulations 2006 provide that the transferor and the transferee are jointly and severally liable for any failure to inform and consult.
- The contracts of employment of all those employed wholly or mainly in the undertaking at the time of the transfer (and who do not object to transferring) transfer automatically to the transferee (you).
- Any changes to terms and conditions of employment for a reason connected with the transfer are invalid even if the employee consents to the change; the only exception is where the reason is an economic, technical or organizational (ETO) reason entailing changes in the workforce.
- Any dismissal made in connection with the transfer will be automatically unfair unless it is for an economic, technical or organizational (ETO) reason entailing changes in the workforce, which broadly means redundancy, or changes in job function, such as a move from a secretarial position to a sales position.

Does the current contractor recognize a trade union in relation to the canteen staff? If so, and if the canteen maintains a distinct identity separate from the rest of your organization, you will also be held to have recognized it so far as the canteen is concerned. And/ or are there collective agreement/s covering the canteen staff? Any such agreements will continue to apply to them.

Longer term, you may wish to bring the terms and conditions of transferred-in canteen staff more into line with the terms and conditions of the rest of your employees. You will, over time, be able to do this – with their agreement – but you will need to be able to demonstrate that the 'sole' or 'principal' reason is not connected with the transfer. The mere passage of time will not, of itself, provide such a demonstration, but the longer ago the transfer is when any such change is made the more difficult it will be to argue maintenance of the link to it. Also, if any change is linked to some other specific cause – for example, an 'annual round' wage negotiation – any presumption of a link with the transfer is more likely to be rebutted.

3.   You will need to look carefully at the position of the catering manager. If the current contractor has an employee in an equivalent position working wholly, or very largely, just on the contract with you it is possible that he or she would be covered by the TUPE transfer. The 'undertaking' transferred might be held to include its specific management structure as well as the 'operational' staff. If so, and you refuse to take him or her on and instead appoint your own replacement, you could be faced with a claim for automatically unfair dismissal. By rejecting him or her you would be dismissing him or her. And a dismissal by reason of, or for a reason connected with, a transfer is automatically unfair unless it is for an ETO reason. A simple wish to change the identity of a particular post-holder is not enough. So, before appointing 'your own new catering manager', you will need to satisfy yourself that such a post is vacant. If there is no one in the current contractor's organization who is dedicated to, and integrated with, the running of your canteen, you should be free to advertise.

4.   You will not be able to change the canteen staff's contracts to make them more mobile, even with their consent, if it is found to be by reason of the transfer. It may be better either to phase this is over the longer term or to 'ring fence' the current staff's terms and conditions but introduce mobility into the contracts for all new staff.

5.   The TUPE Regulations 2006 also introduced a new obligation on the transferor (Grub-at-Work) to provide the transferee (you) with employee liability information. This requires the transferor to notify the transferee in writing of all rights and obligations – anything they 'ought' to know – regarding transferring employees, including their identity. The transferor also has to notify any changes after the information is given.

The information can be given in instalments, or through a third party, in good time before the transfer, although specific deadlines are not given.

Where the transferor has failed to meet this requirement, the transferee can complain to an Employment Tribunal. The Tribunal can award such compensation as is just and equitable in all the circumstances, subject to a minimum of £500 per employee.

? Question

Joe Smith, who worked for a borough council, was dismissed after being employed as a street cleaner for less than one year. On the following day, the council contracted out their street cleaning services.

It was common ground that the transfer came within the Transfer of Undertakings (Protection of Employment) Regulations 2006. Joe lost his job.

Can Joe claim compensation for unfair dismissal?

Solution **!**

It is likely that Joe was dismissed in order to make the contract for the cleaning services more attractive to the incoming contractor who probably did not want to take on the expense of employing Joe. Ordinarily, therefore, Joe's dismissal would be automatically unfair as being related to the TUPE transfer, but because he is not eligible to bring an unfair dismissal claim (as he does not have a year's service), his remedies are limited.

A claim he would have against the incoming contractor (who would have inherited all rights and liabilities attaching to Joe's contract) is a breach of contract/wrongful dismissal claim in the event that he was dismissed without proper notice or without outstanding payments being met, for example holiday pay, by the council.

The council should also have given the new contractor the relevant 'employee liability information' (Reg. 11), which would identify Joe, and any contractual terms, such as notice or holiday pay.

Another possible claim would arise in the event that the council did not consult with Joe about the transfer before it happened. Regulation 13 of the 2006 Regulations places a statutory duty on the council to inform and consult representatives of 'affected employees' about the transfer in good time before the transfer itself. The compensation Joe could receive for such a claim is capped at 13 weeks' pay. This is a liability that would pass under the Regulations to the incoming contractor and which commercially the contractor would have provided for by receiving confirmation from the council that consultation took place and an indemnity in the event that it is found not to have taken place.

Question

Nitrox Ltd, a supplier of diving equipment, has bought a smaller competitor company, Dive 99 Ltd, and has assimilated its sales operation into its own. It has been noted that the sales force from Dive 99 did not have any restrictive covenants. Nitrox issues new contracts to the ex-Dive 99 sales force, which contain a 12-month restriction on dealing with any Nitrox customer.

Peter was Dive 99's top salesman. He signs his new contract, but soon becomes disillusioned with Nitrox, resigns, and sets up his own competing business. He has sent a mail shot to the customers he dealt with.

What can Nitrox do?

Solution

There are two issues here: the effect of TUPE, and the validity of the restrictive covenant.

First, it is clear that TUPE applies and therefore the contracts of employment of all employees of Dive 99 transfer across to Nitrox. Any change to Peter's contract of employment, if it is for a TUPE reason, is null and void, even if he has signed and accepted new terms. On the face of it, the insistence on signing the new restrictive covenant was directly related to TUPE; depending on the circumstances Nitrox may be able to run an argument that the reason for the change was not TUPE related, but was for 'customer protection' reasons; it would have to be able to demonstrate that not only the ex-Dive 99 people received new contracts, but that this was a company-wide process. However, where employers wish to harmonize conditions following a TUPE transfer, it may be difficult to show that this was not a reason connected with the transfer. Peter will therefore be free to ignore the restrictive covenant.

Even if the covenant is not void for TUPE reasons, it is far from certain that a court would uphold it as valid. Restrictive covenants are upheld by the courts only to the extent that they are reasonably necessary to protect proprietary interests of the employer, such as confidential information or its client base. Here, the duration of the restraint, 12 months, seems excessive, although all of the circumstances would need to be investigated to decide if that was an excessive period. What is Peter's salary and his notice period, and how senior is he in the organization?

Generally speaking, a covenant preventing dealing with or solicitation of customers will be enforceable only if it focuses on the actual customers that the individual concerned has dealt with. Here the restriction relates to any Nitrox customer. Since Peter is effectively a new arrival in that company, it is highly likely that Nitrox will have many customers that he has never had any dealings with at all. Therefore a covenant purportedly preventing him from dealing with any Nitrox customer is probably too wide to be enforceable. Any application for an injunction by Nitrox would therefore fail completely; the court has no power to rewrite a covenant and to impose a lesser restriction. The clause stands or falls as drafted.

Question

Mike works as a financial controller in a company that manufactures security systems. He has been working there for five years and receives a salary of £60,000. Pete, the managing director, after conducting a review of the business, decides that he is going to outsource the accounts function to a firm of accountants in an attempt to reduce overheads. He has received a quote from a local firm of accountants who have told him that they could deal with the company management accounts, payroll, VAT and year-end tax for £10,000 per year.

Pete, therefore, informs Mike that his position may be at risk of redundancy and invites him to a meeting to discuss the situation. During the meeting, Mike explains that if the majority of his work is going to be outsourced he should be transferred under TUPE to the firm of accountants who take on the contract. Pete is worried about this since he feels that the firm of accountants will refuse to take on the contract if Mike is transferred with it.

Is Mike correct in stating that TUPE applies to the situation? How should Pete deal with this?

Solution

The Transfer of Undertakings (Protection of Employment) Regulations 2006 (TUPE) apply only where there is a 'relevant transfer'. Prior to the 2006 Regulations this had to involve the transfer of 'an economic entity which retains its identity'. Case law had already recognized that the provision of a service might involve such an entity, but as a result of the 2006 Regulations the definition was expanded expressly to cover 'service provision changes'. For present purposes the relevant part of that definition is: 'where activities cease to be carried out by a person ("a client") on his own behalf and are carried out instead by another person on the client's behalf ("a contractor")'.

The only other condition that is relevant for present purposes is that: 'immediately before the service provision change [...] there is an organized grouping of employees [...] which has as its principal purpose the carrying out of the activities concerned on behalf of the client'.

In order to apply that law any Tribunal would first have to determine, as matters of fact, what actually happened before and after any purported transfer. What the Tribunal would have to do would be identify the 'activities'. So, in this case, it would need to look at what the accountancy firm was doing after the 'transfer' which had been done before the 'transfer' by Mike. Having identified the 'activities' being 'transferred', the Tribunal would then have to decide, as a matter of fact, whether there was, before the 'transfer', an organized grouping of employees which had as its principal purpose the carrying out of those activities.

A single employee can constitute 'an organized grouping of employees', and working on the assumption that Mike is an 'organized grouping', the Tribunal would need to assess whether Mike's 'principal purpose' was to undertake the 'activities' concerned. If all, or most, of the activities originally handled by the organized grouping (ie Mike) were passed to the accountants then the 'principal purpose' test may be satisfied. But if what was passed to the accountancy firm comprised only some of the activities originally undertaken by the organized grouping then, if you reorganized how the other activities were handled internally, the 'principal purpose' test would not be met.

Further, it is fundamentally unlikely that a service which an external contractor can offer to provide for £10,000 per annum could have constituted those activities which were the 'principal purpose' of an employee being paid a total package of almost £60,000 per annum. Both Mike's title and his salary level suggest that he fulfilled some sort of managerial or professional role: both the list of activities being outsourced and the price quoted for them suggest that they are bookkeeping or number-crunching.

If TUPE does apply, Mike would then transfer to the accountants. That firm is able to make redundancies if there is an economic, technical or organizational reason for doing so. Quite clearly, taking Mike on at a package close to £60,000 with a contract to perform £10,000 worth of work makes no sense, so it is likely that the accountancy firm would make Mike redundant within a week or two, paying his statutory redundancy. So even if TUPE did apply, he wouldn't gain anything from it.

Chapter 4

Redundancy and restructuring

❓ Question

It has been announced that a department is to close down, with all staff being redundant, in six months' time. John has got another job and wants to leave now. He asks if he will still be entitled to his redundancy payment.

Is he?

Solution ❗

In order to qualify for a statutory redundancy payment, an employee has to be *dismissed*. Here, if the contract is terminated at the earlier date that John wants, it will have been terminated by John, not by the employer. That will not, under the normal rules, be a 'dismissal'. The announcement by an employer of an impending redundancy does not involve any breach by the employer of any term in John's contract, so John could not argue that he had been 'constructively' dismissed.

There is, however, a special rule which can preserve the entitlement to a statutory redundancy payment of an employee who leaves early. It is in section 136(3) of the Employment Rights Act 1996. To benefit under this rule the employee first has to have been given notice of dismissal by reason of redundancy by the employer. It is not clear, in this case, whether that has been done. A distinction is drawn between, on the one hand, a general warning that dismissal/s will occur at some future date and, on the other, the giving of notice to terminate a specific contract at some specific date. It is only if John has already personally been given notice to terminate his contract on a precise future date that this provision could operate.

If he has, the next question is whether that notice is longer than is legally required. John's contract of employment will include – expressly or by implication – provisions about the notice necessary to terminate it. If it says nothing else, then the statutory minimum provisions will probably be applied: one week per year of service up to a maximum of twelve weeks' notice for twelve or more years' service. That period, whether it is set out in the contract or derived from the statute, is known as the 'obligatory period of notice' and it runs so as to end on the same date as the notice that was actually given will end. This means that, if it is shorter than the notice that was actually given, it will not start until some way through that period. If John was given, and was actually entitled to, six months' notice then the obligatory period of notice has already started. But if, although actually given six months' notice, he was entitled to (say) only twelve weeks' notice, the obligatory period of notice will not start for another three months or so: it will be the last twelve weeks before the termination date set by the employer.

This is important because the special rule, preserving an early leaver's right to a statutory redundancy payment, operates only where the employee gives notice to the employer within the obligatory period of notice. If John were to leave before the start of the obligatory period of notice, or to give notice before the start of the obligatory period (even if he did not leave until the obligatory period had commenced), or leave without notice after the obligatory period had started, he would forfeit any right to a statutory redundancy payment. But if, once the obligatory period has started, John gives notice to terminate his contract of employment on a date earlier than the employer's notice would expire, he will remain entitled to a statutory redundancy payment unless the employer serves a counter-notice on him.

A counter-notice would have to be served before the notice given by John expired. It is [s.142(2)] a notice in writing: a) requiring the employee to withdraw his notice terminating the contract of employment and to continue in employment until the date on which the employer's notice terminating the contract expires, and b) stating that, unless he does so, the employer will contest any liability to pay to him a redundancy payment in respect of the termination of his contract of employment.

If such a counter-notice is issued, and John still leaves early, he might still be entitled to some or all of a statutory redundancy payment. This is because he can apply to a Tribunal to award such proportion of the payment as is 'just and equitable' having regard [s.142(3)] to: a) the reasons for which the employee seeks to leave the employment, and b) the reasons for which the employer requires him to continue in it.

So far as any contractual, as opposed to statutory, redundancy payment entitlement is concerned, that will depend on the precise terms of John's contract.

Question

A redundancy situation has arisen in your IT department. You have carried out a full and fair redundancy selection procedure and the lowest scorer was Derek. You are worried because Derek is one of those employees with an entire drawer to himself in the personnel filing cabinet and he has always made it clear that he would take the organization to an Employment Tribunal if he were ever dismissed. Therefore, your procedure has to be watertight.

Will the statutory DDP apply to Derek's dismissal by reason of redundancy? How can you ensure your procedure complies with the statutory DDP?

Solution

When thinking about the statutory DDP, it is easy to forget that it applies not only to disciplinary-related dismissals but also to a wide range of other dismissals, including redundancies.

According to the DTI, the statutory DDP is a basic three-step procedure:

1. Write it down.
2. Hold a meeting.
3. Allow the employee to appeal.

If you follow a standard redundancy procedure (selecting the person to be made redundant, informing them that they have provisionally been chosen for redundancy and then allowing them a consultation period in which to challenge their selection for redundancy and/or discuss ways of avoiding the redundancy by – for example – looking for alternative employment, etc), you should comply with those three basic steps.

However, there is a risk that, if Derek does challenge his dismissal and the Tribunal looks at the strict wording of the DDP, you may not comply with the full technical requirements of the DDP. These are:

1. The employer must set out in writing the employee's alleged conduct or characteristics, or other circumstances, which led it to contemplate dismissal.

2. The employer must send the statement to the employee and ask him or her to a meeting ('Meeting One') to discuss the matter.
3. The meeting must take place before any action is taken.
4. The meeting must not take place unless:
   a. the employer has informed the employee of the basis or grounds for contemplating dismissal;
   b. the employee has had a reasonable opportunity to consider his or her response to that information.
5. After the meeting, the employer must inform the employee of its decision and notify him or her of the right to appeal against it if he or she is not satisfied with it.
6. If the employee does wish to appeal, he or she must inform the employer and the employer must invite him or her to attend a further meeting ('Meeting Two').
7. After the appeal meeting, the employer must inform the employee of its decision.

The question is: Where does this procedure fit into a standard redundancy procedure?

Under a standard redundancy procedure, you would meet with Derek to tell him that he has been provisionally selected for redundancy and start a consultation period. You would probably meet with Derek once or twice during the consultation period to talk about alternative vacancies or give Derek a chance to challenge the redundancy. At the end of the consultation period, if nothing had changed, you would give Derek notice of termination on the grounds of redundancy. Fitting this series of meetings around the DDP is not all that easy.

If you make the first meeting with Derek Meeting One, then, in order to comply with the DDP, you will have to write to Derek with full details of the redundancy and the reasons and grounds for his provisional selection for redundancy prior to that meeting (Step 1 and Step 4(a)). In reality, you may not want to do that.

In *Alexander* v. *Brigden Enterprises Ltd* (2006) the Employment Appeal Tribunal (EAT) indicated that Step 1, in a redundancy situation, only requires the employer to set out the issue in broad terms, which may involve no more than telling the employee that he is at risk of dismissal by reason of redundancy. It is at Step 2, the meeting, that the employee must be informed of the basis for those grounds, and this will involve an explanation as to why you are contemplating dismissing Derek for redundancy. This will involve information as to why there is a redundancy situation, and why Derek has been provisionally selected. In order to comply with Step 2, the EAT said that the employee should be notified in advance of that meeting of the selection criteria that have been used, and also the assessment of the employee. This then gives the employee the opportunity at the meeting 'to make representations not only about whether the criteria are appropriate and justified, but also, more importantly, whether the marking given to him in respect of any particular criterion is arguably unjust and why'. Failure to do this leads to the dismissal being automatically unfair.

In addition, under the DDP, you must inform Derek of your decision *after* Meeting One (Step 5). If you go into Meeting One having told Derek in writing all of the reasons why he is being provisionally selected for redundancy, what 'decision' are you informing him of *after* the meeting? You would have to allow Derek to comment on the provisional selection at Meeting One and then tell him after that meeting: 'Despite your representations, you are still provisionally selected for redundancy; you do have the right to appeal against this decision if you want to' (Step 5).

If Derek did appeal, you would then have to hold an appeal meeting (Step 6), but in reality you would probably do this anyway.

Alternatively, you could go through the normal redundancy procedure and then make the final meeting (the one at which Derek is given his notice of redundancy) Meeting One. This would probably ensure that Steps 1 to 4 were complied with. However, under Step 5, you would have to then offer Derek a *further* appeal. If Derek did appeal, you would have to hold a further appeal meeting. This is over and above the requirements of a normal redundancy procedure.

If you do not want to do this, one option may be to make one of your consultation meetings (which you would be having anyway as part of a fair redundancy procedure) your Meeting One. This would work thus:

1. Invite Derek to a meeting as normal, at which you can explain the redundancy situation and explain why he has been provisionally selected for redundancy.
2. Write to Derek, setting out everything that was said at that meeting, including the reason why you are contemplating dismissing Derek by reason of redundancy. Include in that letter the structure charts or any other justification for the redundancy and also his scores from the selection matrix and the names of the other people included in the pool with him (Step 1).
3. Invite Derek to a meeting to discuss this (Step 2, Meeting One).
4. At that meeting (at which Derek has the right to be accompanied by a colleague or trade union representative), you will allow Derek to give representations on his provisional selection for redundancy.

5. After the meeting, you should write to Derek saying that, despite his representations, he is still provisionally selected for redundancy and notifying him of the right to appeal against that decision if he wants to (Step 5).
6. [Throughout all of this, you should still be actively looking for alternative jobs for Derek.]
7. If Derek does appeal, then an appeal meeting must be held (Step 6). After that meeting, Derek should be told of the final decision (Step 7). After Derek has been told that his appeal has been unsuccessful and that, despite his representations, he is still provisionally selected for redundancy, you can then go on to serve him with notice of redundancy.

Conducting the meetings in this way in order to comply with the statutory DDP is a bit of a farce and we would hope that Tribunals will be sensible enough to take a reasonably flexible approach to the technical requirements of the DDP in cases where an otherwise fair redundancy procedure has been followed.

However, the law as it stands is that a technical breach of the DDP can render an otherwise fair dismissal automatically unfair so, in the case of employees like Derek, it may be worth ensuring you comply with the letter, as well as the spirit, of the DTI's 'Simple as 1,2,3...' procedure.

Question

Pie In The Sky Ltd is an airline catering business, providing in-flight meals for a number of short- and long-haul carriers. Over the years the company has grown in a haphazard way, with a multi-layered management and supervisory structure. As the new HR manager, you are asked to implement a restructuring.

Although there are various dimensions to this restructuring, for the purposes of this question we will concentrate on the following aspect. You establish that the roles of senior supervisor, supervisor, and charge hand have similarities, and you decide to abolish those three job titles and replace them with a new team leader post.

Business for Pie In The Sky is reasonably good and static. However, rather than 30 employees occupying supervisory/charge hand positions, you decide that the operation can be run efficiently with 20 team leaders. The new team leader position is closest to the old supervisory position. As far as the senior supervisors are concerned, they will lose some degree of responsibility for the management of airline contracts, and some staff management responsibilities, as well as a perceived, if slight, drop in status. Charge hands would take on greater responsibilities if they were appointed to the team leader position. The earnings for the three positions are £23,000 to £25,000 for senior supervisors, £20,000 to £23,000 for supervisors, and £18,000 to £20,000 for charge hands. The salary for the team leader position is a fixed £20,000, with limited opportunities for overtime.

What issues arise, and what is the correct sequence of events as you set about this restructuring?

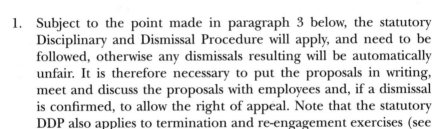

Solution

A number of legal issues arise in dealing with this scenario, which are as follows:

1. Subject to the point made in paragraph 3 below, the statutory Disciplinary and Dismissal Procedure will apply, and need to be followed, otherwise any dismissals resulting will be automatically unfair. It is therefore necessary to put the proposals in writing, meet and discuss the proposals with employees and, if a dismissal is confirmed, to allow the right of appeal. Note that the statutory DDP also applies to termination and re-engagement exercises (see paragraph 5 below).
2. General principles of unfair dismissal still apply, and observation of the statutory DDP will not, of itself, render a dismissal fair.
3. On the face of the numbers, 10 people will be leaving the organization, not enough to trigger the rules on collective consultation. However, in *Scotch Premier* v. *Burns* (2000), it was decided that in the context of the collective consultation rules, the definition of the word 'redundancy' is very wide and includes not just a situation where employees are redundant in the classic sense, but also any situation in which there may be a 'no fault' dismissal, followed by re-engagement under a new contract. One way or another, the 30 employees will not be carrying on with their old supervisory/charge hand job titles, and whilst only 10 will be leaving the organization completely, there is nonetheless a legal requirement to follow a collective consultation process.

    Given the above, it may be the case that the statutory DDP does not apply – one of the exclusions is where there is a collective consultation exercise. However, the recommended approach is still to follow the statutory minimum, to avoid any possible challenge in this area.

4. You need to consider whether the restructuring process is a variation of contract exercise, or a redundancy exercise. Where only parts of a contract are to be changed, and no fundamental terms will be affected, then the exercise is probably a variation of contract. This might arise, for example, where a new shift system is to be introduced requiring employees to work altered hours, but in all other respects duties and pay remain the same. By contrast, where there are significant alterations to the contract, such as a reduction in pay or the reallocation of significant responsibilities, then the legal analysis may be that the old position is redundant and the new post is offered by the company on the basis of its being a suitable alternative (see below).

5. If the variations are towards the minor end of the scale, rendering it a contract variation exercise rather than redundancy, the correct process, briefly, is as follows. Consult with the employees and endeavour to secure their agreement to sign new contracts. If that agreement is not forthcoming, the employer can then serve notice under the old contract and, at the same time, offer up a new contract on the revised terms. This is known as termination and re-engagement. If an employee declines to sign the new contract and leaves at the end of the notice period, and subsequently claims unfair dismissal, the employer's defence is based on the 'some other substantial reason' fair reason to dismiss. Provided the employer has a sound business reason for making the change, and has consulted properly, a fair dismissal will result.

6. In the Pie in the Sky restructure, the changes are fairly significant, and the advisable approach is to accept that the 30 supervisory/charge hand posts are redundant. The company's position will then be that the team leader posts are suitable alternatives. In considering alternative job offers, there is a two-stage process. First, on an objective basis, is the post indeed a suitable alternative? Are the responsibilities, job content, status and payment comparable? Although each case is decided individually, by way of example in one decided authority, a pay reduction of 15 per cent meant that the Tribunal decided that it was not a suitable alternative.

    The second limb of the process is whether, assuming the post is a suitable alternative, the employee was reasonable in refusing it. This is a subjective test and will be influenced by the employee's personal circumstances. For example, if the suitable alternative involves a relocation which is inconvenient to the employee because he or she does not drive, then it might be reasonable to turn down the suitable alternative.

If an employee unreasonably refuses a suitable alternative, then he or she is disqualified from statutory redundancy pay. His or her employment will still end by reason of redundancy, but without the obligation on the employee to pay statutory redundancy.

In the case of Pie in the Sky, it is unlikely that the team leader position will be a suitable alternative for senior supervisors, but may be for supervisors. Therefore if senior supervisors do not want to accept the alternative role, they are entitled to statutory redundancy.

An employee is entitled to accept a suitable alternative on the basis of a statutory trial period which lasts up to four weeks. If, during that period, the employee decides that he or she does not want to take the position, he or she can then claim his or her statutory redundancy and leave. This is on the proviso that it is reasonable for the employee not to accept the suitable alternative, as described in the paragraph above. Trial periods can be extended by mutual agreement.

7. Given that there are 20 positions and 30 members of staff, if more than 20 wish to pursue the suitable alternatives, then a redundancy selection exercise will need to be established under which the best candidates are selected for the available posts.

Question

Your company has experienced a prolonged downturn in business, forcing you to conclude that you need to restructure the company and reduce the workforce.

You wish to start with your 'management team' and have received conflicting ideas on the correct approach. One friend recommended making a paper selection where everyone scores against a matrix and the worst scorers go whilst the survivors automatically fill the new jobs. A former colleague suggests asking everyone to apply for the new jobs and requiring them to make a presentation and attend an interview.

Is one method preferable or perhaps an amalgam of the two? What would you do?

Solution

First, it is essential to identify whether you are restructuring or making redundancies. Whilst a restructure often does lead to redundancies, a dismissal in such circumstances is for 'some other substantial reason', not redundancy. This can be very important if the dismissal is later challenged.

Second, analyse your team. As well as 'managing', a management team often covers such specialisms as operations, finance, marketing and human resources. Consider what functions need to be discharged under the new regime and then how those functions can be combined into new jobs. A comparison of the new picture with the existing one might show, for example, that the finance group is overstaffed by four, whereas marketing must remain unaffected.

In practice, whether your decision is that you are restructuring or making redundancies it will probably lead to the same result, but the 'technical' approach has two distinct advantages: 1) the closer what actually happens is to the conceptual framework against which actions and decisions will be judged, the easier it usually is to defend those actions and decisions; 2) it can help to identify the most appropriate 'selection' method for implementing the change.

It is suggested that a matrix is more appropriate for a true 'redundancy' whereas applying for jobs is more appropriate for 'reorganization'. Where there is little change in the duties/functions of each job, the only difference being numbers, there is a redundancy leading to selection for dismissal from the old jobs. Where the 'new' jobs comprise different collections of duties/functions, there is reorganization: all the old jobs are redundant and selection is for the new jobs.

It can be seen from this that different approaches for different circumstances can be justified and thus may well be more acceptable to a Tribunal. An amalgam of the two approaches is therefore not recommended.

However, a final suggestion, in cases where there would seem to be a choice between the two approaches, is to determine which by consultation with the affected employees. This would immeasurably help to meet any subsequent challenge to the methodology.

It is also important to bear in mind the need to follow the statutory dismissal procedures: in *Alexander and Hatherley* v. *Brigden Enterprises* (2005) the EAT ruled that in redundancy dismissals, where a matrix system is used, at Step 2 (the hearing) the employee must be told what the selection criteria are, and what score he or she has achieved, though he or she does not need to be told the threshold score needed to stay in employment, or the scores of other employees. Otherwise, the dismissal will be automatically unfair.

Again, for any redundancy dismissals involving fewer than 20 dismissals within a 90-day period, you must ensure the statutory procedures are followed. For large-scale redundancies, you need to follow the collective consultation procedures. It would also be a good idea to follow the collective consultation procedures if you choose to ask 20+ people to reapply for jobs, as there is a possibility that you will be dismissing some or all of them at the end of the process.

? Question

International Rescue runs an air ambulance service, with aircraft, equipment and 40 operational employees based at a small airfield, and with 30 sales and administrative staff in a town about eight miles away. The sudden loss of a major contract means significant job cuts; 15 at the airfield and 10 at the admin centre. The HR manager, under pressure to act quickly, uses a skills matrix from his previous job, which managers apply to employees in their departments.

A week later the names of those to be made redundant are announced. A disgruntled employee asks to see the scores of all redundant employees.

What issues may arise here?

Solution !

Where there are to be 20 or more redundancies at one establishment within a 90-day period, collective consultation rules apply. Whether or not that will be the case here depends on the 'same establishment' issue. If the airfield and the admin centre, which are only eight miles apart, can be regarded as one establishment, then clearly the employer is exposed to claims for protective awards from all redundant employees. The key test in determining whether or not there is one establishment is consideration of where the employees are assigned to perform their duties. If there is a lot of interchange between the two establishments, with some employees effectively working at both, and others being transferred backwards and forwards regularly, then there is a danger that the airfield and the admin centre could be regarded as one establishment. However, that appears to be unlikely in this case as the operational people clearly have a different function to the admin people, and whilst there will naturally be a degree of interchange, employees will in the main be assigned to one location or the other. Therefore the collective consultation rules probably do not apply here. However, the employer will need to follow the statutory Disciplinary and Dismissal Procedure.

In *Alexander and Hatherley* v. *Brigden Enterprises* (2005) the EAT ruled that in redundancy dismissals, where a matrix system is used, at Step 2 (the hearing) the employee must be told what the selection criteria are, and what score he or she has achieved, though he or she does not need to be told the threshold score needed to stay in employment, or the scores of other employees. Otherwise, the dismissal will be automatically unfair.

Simply finding a skills matrix and applying it, whilst creating to some extent the impression of a properly executed redundancy exercise, is flawed. There appears to have been little consultation here, and part of that consultation should be consideration of the skills matrix, that is, putting the draft matrix out for discussion and taking employees' view on how it should be implemented.

If a redundancy exercise is implemented without consideration of the relevant pools, then all dismissals are likely to be rendered unfair. In this case the managers have simply applied the skills matrix to their departments. This can often be a simple and tempting course of action; departmental applications may be appropriate in some cases, but it is often a requirement that pools are interdepartmental and considered in a wider context. For example, secretarial and support staff right across the business would be regarded as being in one pool, regardless of the department that they are working in.

Generally, employees are entitled to see only their own scores, and not those of others within the business. That, however, presupposes that the Tribunal accepts that in broad terms the process was a proper and fair one, reasonably applied. Where the Tribunal believes that the whole process was flawed and entirely ineffective, there is a danger that the ambit of documentation disclosure could be wider.

Question

Masters and Masters supplied cattle feeders to farmers in the UK and, following a string of various agricultural disasters, were finding it hard to make ends meet. They had looked at possibly diversifying, but could come up only with other products aimed at the same market, so eventually decided that the only thing to do was to make a few redundancies. Masters and Masters saw the redundancy situation as an opportunity to get rid of some employees who had the reputation of being troublemakers, including some employees who have been muttering about unions and some who are members, so adapted the criteria for selection for redundancy accordingly. There were also one or two other opportunities within the organization, but these were not discussed with any of the 'at risk' employees.

Was the redundancy handled correctly?

Solution !

As Masters and Masters are looking to make 'a few' redundancies there can be an assumption that the collective consultation obligations will not come into play as they involve redundancies of over 20 people. We therefore have a situation of individual consultation and the fair process that goes with that. The DDP must be complied with.

Guidelines for a fair redundancy procedure were given by the Employment Appeal Tribunal in *Williams* v. *Compair Maxam Ltd* (1982). These were:

1. The employer will seek to give as much warning as possible of impending redundancies.
2. The employer will consult with the union regarding the procedure and especially with regard to selection (collective consultation).
3. Whether or not an agreement as to the criteria to be adopted has been agreed with the union, the employer will seek to establish criteria for selection which so far as possible do not depend solely upon the opinion of the person making the selection, but can be objectively checked against such things as attendance record, efficiency at the job, experience or length of service.
4. The employer will seek to ensure that the selection is made fairly.
5. The employer will seek to see whether, instead of dismissing an employee, it could offer him alternative employment.

Although this case involved an employer where a union was recognized, the same basic principles apply where the employer does not recognize a union. Where an employer omits one of the stages above, it will not automatically lead to an unfair procedure, although it is likely to do so.

Taking these steps into account, it would appear that the way Masters and Masters is fixing its selection criteria will not make for a fair procedure. In practical terms, however, the Tribunal cannot substitute its own view for the employer's view and so if it 'appears' that the selection criteria are fair and relevant, without compelling evidence to show otherwise, a Tribunal would probably accept the criteria. Apart from the selection criteria of last in first out, most selection matrices work by disposing of the weakest employees – whether this be in terms of productivity, attendance, disciplinary records, team playing etc. So, getting rid of 'troublemakers' may be the natural result of fair and relevant criteria.

It is automatically unfair to select employees for redundancy for a reason relating to their membership of a union, or their participation in union activities. It is debatable if 'mutterings' can be regarded as participation in union activities, but it is clearly a danger zone.

With regard to alternative employment, an employer who fails to offer suitable alternative employment, or discuss other possibilities of employment, will be acting unreasonably, thereby rendering the dismissal unfair. In all but the smallest companies the employer should be able to demonstrate that it has considered alternative employment and discussed it with the employee. Otherwise there is likely to be a breach of the overriding test of fairness set out in the Employment Rights Act 1996 s98 (4):

> the determination of the question whether the dismissal is fair or unfair (having regard to the reason shown by the employer) (a) depends on whether in the circumstances (including the size and administrative resources of the employer's undertaking) the employer acted reasonably or unreasonably in treating it as a sufficient reason for dismissing the employee....

See also pages 150, 166 and 190.

Chapter 5

Consultation

Question

One of your employees, Bob, requests a meeting with you. At that meeting Bob tells you that he wants an Information and Consultation Committee set up for the company. Bob further tells you that because of the rules for establishing voluntary committees, you have to comply with the statutory provisions and that this process should begin immediately. Bob threatens to make a complaint to the Tribunal if you don't take action immediately.

Do you have to take any action? If you don't, is Bob able to make a complaint to the Tribunal?

Solution

Bob is referring to the Information and Consultation of Employees Regulations 2004, which came into effect on 6 April 2005. The Regulations give employees the right to be consulted about the business's economic situation, informed and consulted about employment prospects, and informed and consulted about decisions likely to lead to substantial changes in the work organization or contractual relations, including redundancies and transfers.

Whether or not you need to take any action at all will first depend upon the number of employees your company has. The Regulations applied only to companies with 150 or more employees from 2005. This will gradually be extended to smaller companies from 2007 onwards.

At the moment you are only aware of a single request that has been made by Bob. Clearly if your workforce is over 150 employees, Bob will not constitute 10 per cent of it. This is relevant because until 10 per cent of the workforce makes a request to establish the Information and Consultation Committee you still do not have to take any action. If you have a pre-existing agreement on consultation, such as a collective bargaining arrangement with a trade union that meets the strict criteria laid down in the Regulations, then Bob will need the backing of 40 per cent of the workforce to trigger the procedures; you can choose instead to ballot all your employees to see if they endorse the request.

Let us assume that Bob does have the backing of 10 per cent of the workforce and that there are no pre-existing agreements; what action must be taken then? The request has been made after the Regulations have come into force and therefore the opportunity to establish an Information and Consultation Committee voluntarily has also passed. You will therefore have to comply with the statutory provisions for the committee.

You will have to ballot the entire workforce to elect employee representatives to stand on the new committee, which must be established within six months of the request. You must then comply with the statutory provisions for providing the employee representatives with information and thereafter consult with these representatives on those matters as outlined above.

Will Bob be able to make a complaint to the Employment Tribunal?

If you have 149 employees or fewer, Bob has no grounds for complaint if no action is taken. If you have 150 employees or more and the 10 per cent threshold is not reached within six months of the initial employee request, Bob has no grounds for complaint if no action is taken.

If you have 150 employees and the 10 per cent threshold is established and no action is taken, Bob will not be able to make a claim to the Employment Tribunal. Bob will, however, be able to make a complaint to the Central Arbitration Committee (CAC) in relation to the company's failure to act upon the employees' request. This could result in an order being made by the CAC that the company rectify the situation and the company could be fined up to £75,000 if it fails to do so.

See also pages 61, 74 and 79.

Chapter 6

Data protection

? Question

Your company obtains a contract to supply services to a pharma-ceutical company. You have advertised for a delivery driver to help you to service that contract and have received an application from Dave, who seems the most suitable candidate for the job. However, you have also received a tip-off that Dave has a history as a militant animal rights activist, and you are worried about his motives in applying. You want to carry out some checks into his past.

What can you do?

Solution !

There are two issues here. One is whether it would be lawful for you to turn down an applicant for employment on the grounds that he had been (or you believed he had been) involved in anti-vivisectionist groups or activities. The other is whether you are entitled, anyway, to investigate whether there had been any such involvement.

The two are separate, but to some extent interlinked. If it would not be lawful for you to turn an applicant down on these grounds then – even if you were entitled to investigate the matter – it might be dangerous to do so, as it would highlight to the applicant that you were expressly collecting information on which, he or she could later claim, reliance in your decision making would be unlawful.

Even if it would be lawful for you to turn an applicant down on these grounds, this would not automatically make it lawful for you to collect information on the subject. The relevant legal provisions are the Employment Equality (Religion or Belief) Regulations 2003 and the Data Protection Act 1998.

Religious or belief discrimination

It became unlawful from December 2003 to discriminate in offers of employment on the grounds of 'religion or belief' (under the Employment Equality (Religion or Belief) Regulations 2003). The definition of 'religion or belief' was amended in 2006 so that 'belief' means any religious or political belief: there is no longer a requirement that a philosophical belief must be similar to a religious belief. This makes it more possible, though still not likely, that anti-vivisection could amount to a philosophical belief. On balance, the odds are probably against such a finding. The pragmatic question is whether you are prepared to take that risk. If you are not, then you should not ask any questions about or initiate any other investigations of Dave's involvement in anti-vivisectionist groups or activities, or give any other reason for Dave to think that such involvement may influence your recruitment decisions.

However, if Dave's motives in applying for this job are to cause trouble, that is potentially a serious issue. If you are prepared to take the risk of Dave making a claim of religious or philosophical belief discrimination, you should be completely open about what you are doing and why. This is because covert investigations into a person's political or religious beliefs without their knowledge or consent will constitute a breach of the Data Protection Act.

Data Protection Act

If you feel that the potential risks justify you in carrying out pre-employment vetting, you should consider the advice given in the Employment Practices Code, Part 1 – recruitment and selection, issued by the Information Commissioner. This will be taken into account in any legal proceedings under the Data Protection Act.

Information about Dave's anti-vivisectionist beliefs or activities is 'sensitive personal data'. This means that, before you can legally process it (including asking an agent to investigate it), you must have the data subject's explicit permission.

Therefore, if possible, you should expressly ask all the applicants – ideally on an application form that they are given at interview so that both the question and the answer are in writing – something on the lines of: 'Have you ever been involved in any anti-vivisectionist groups or activities?' On the same form, you should let the applicants know that you will carry out checks to confirm the accuracy of any information they have given you as part of the recruitment exercise. If you then did ask an agent to investigate Dave's background, it would be no different in principle from, for example, checking to see if a candidate's claims to particular academic qualifications were correct.

Conclusion

In summary, it is an 'either/or' situation. Either you take the stance that you would be entitled to refuse an applicant with an anti-vivisectionist background, in which case, in order to cover yourself under the Data Protection Act, you will need to be transparent about the information you are collecting.

Or, if you are not prepared to risk the possibility of a discrimination claim under the Employment Equality (Religion or Belief) Regulations 2003, you would have no legitimate reason to collect such sensitive personal data. To do so openly would simply invite such a claim. To do so covertly would involve breach of the Data Protection Act.

Question

Peter comes to you with a grievance against Hamish, who he says has been making racially harassing comments against him. Peter produces some tapes, which he says are secret recordings that he has made of Hamish in the workplace.

Hamish has got to know about these tapes and is furious about Peter's actions. He says that, if the material is used in any way, he will take action against the organization for breaching his privacy under the Data Protection Act.

Can you, and should you, listen to those tapes and use them in dealing with this grievance, and is there any action that Hamish can take against you if you do, and – on the basis of the information on the tapes – dismiss him?

Solution

Data Protection Act 1998

The Data Protection Act 1998 (DPA) does not create a free-standing right to privacy. Rather it creates rights and imposes duties with respect to the handling and the use of 'data'. The Data Protection Code on Employee Monitoring itself states: 'The covert observation of workers is not in itself subject to the DPA, but once it results in records being kept about individual workers, the Act will apply.'

The Act will apply only if the records themselves are qualifying 'data' under the DPA. Not all information is 'data' under the DPA. In order to qualify as 'data', and so be covered by the DPA, information must be:

1. processed by automatic equipment; or
2. recorded with the intention of such processing; or
3. recorded in, or with the intention that it should go in, a relevant filing system (ie a computerized system or a manual system that is as sophisticated as a computerized system (*Durrant* v. *FSA* [2003] EWCA Civ 1746).

It is hard to see how a tape recording could be such a system.

In any event, the DPA would apply only if the information contained on the tapes is 'personal data'. Again, the case of *Durrant* v. *FSA* provided some guidance on what constituted 'personal data'. Effectively, information is only 'personal data' if it is data that affects a person's privacy, whether in his or her personal or family life, business or professional capacity.

Again, it is hard to see how a recording of Hamish harassing Peter could be seen as 'personal data' about Hamish. Therefore, it is highly unlikely that the Data Protection Act will apply here at all.

Even if it did apply, it would only really give Hamish a claim against Peter himself. Peter is the person who made the tapes and is therefore the 'data controller'. The DPA would allow Hamish to make a subject access request to Peter or try to bring some court action against Hamish or apply to the Information Commissioner for an enforcement notice against Hamish if he feels that Hamish has breached one of the Data Protection Principles. These are:

1. Data must be fairly and lawfully processed.
2. Data must be processed for limited purposes.
3. Data must be adequate, relevant and not excessive.
4. Data must be accurate.
5. Data must not be kept for longer than necessary.
6. Data must be processed in accordance with the data subject's rights.
7. Data must be kept secure.
8. Data must not be transferred to countries outside the EEA without adequate protection.

The DPA would not give Hamish any claims against the organization in this case.

Race harassment investigations

You would be well advised to take Peter's evidence seriously, as employers are vicariously liable for the actions of their employees under the Race Relations Act 1976. If Peter brings a race discrimination claim, the only defence the organization will be able to put up (assuming that Hamish did make the remarks that Peter has accused him of) is that it took all reasonable steps to prevent that harassment from taking place.

Therefore, if you refuse to take action based on these tapes, you may well risk an extremely serious discrimination claim being brought against the organization by Peter further down the line.

Dismissing Hamish

Determination of whether a dismissal is fair or unfair depends (under s98 of the Employment Rights Act 1996) on the reason for the dismissal and whether the employer acted reasonably or unreasonably in treating that as a sufficient reason for dismissing the employee.

In this case, Hamish might try to argue that the organization acted unreasonably in using the tapes as part of its investigation, but this line of argument will only really benefit him if he can show that the use of the tapes breached his right to privacy.

Right to privacy

If Hamish brought an unfair dismissal claim against you, he might try to argue that there has been a breach of Article 8 of the Human Rights Act (HRA) (1998), the right to privacy, by these secret recordings. The HRA has direct effect only on public sector organizations. Assuming that this is a private sector employer, the HRA will not apply. The HRA nonetheless has impact in Tribunal proceedings. The Tribunal is in the public sector and is bound by s6 of the HRA not to act in a way that is incompatible with a Convention right.

If a Tribunal believes that evidence has been obtained which is in breach of the HRA, it can make an order that this evidence is disregarded. Since in this particular case the disciplinary hearing and subsequent dismissal seem largely to rest on the information in the tapes, if the employer is not allowed to use that information, the effect of such a decision by the Tribunal would be to strike out their defence and the employee would in effect win by default.

However, the right to privacy afforded by Article 8 is not absolute. It competes against other articles, including Article 10 (freedom of expression) and, more importantly in this case, Article 6 (the right to a fair trial).

In the case of *Jones* v. *University of Warwick* (2003), a private enquiry agent covertly video-recorded a woman in her own home in order to demonstrate that her movements were not as restricted as her insurance claim made out. The Court of Appeal held that, while to admit such evidence before a court or tribunal might infringe the claimant's right to privacy, to exclude it would jeopardize the defendant's right to a fair trial. Therefore, the court said, insofar as the defendant's actions (or those of its agent) were reprehensible, that should not lead to the exclusion of the evidence but should be reflected in any costs award.

In *McGowan* v. *Scottish Water* (2005) the Employment Appeal Tribunal (EAT) held that covert surveillance of an employee's home was justified, where he was suspected of falsifying timesheets. This was not a breach of his Article 8 rights, as the surveillance was not a disproportionate response in the light of the employer's suspicions.

In addition, the tape recording – assuming it has not been doctored – is no more than corroborative evidence of what Peter and Hamish (if both were telling the truth) could/would say in oral evidence anyway. It is 'best evidence': in Hamish's defence as well as in support of Peter's accusations. For example, if Hamish says he was being 'set up' – goaded into racially hurtful remarks – the tape (perhaps with other evidence that Hamish can bring) should corroborate that as well.

So although it is theoretically possible that an EAT could refuse to admit evidence obtained in breach of privacy, it would be highly unlikely in this case.

See also page 110.

? Question

A troublesome employee writes to you asking for a complete copy of his personal file. On checking, you see a number of 'highly confidential' notes written by various managers, complaining about the employee and asking you to get rid of him. The managers do not want these memos and e-mails disclosed.

Are you obliged to disclose the file? Are you entitled to 'weed out' the bits you don't like?

Solution

Under the Data Protection Act 1998 the information contained on an employee's personal file is '"personal data" if it is recorded on computer, or in manual files which are a relevant filing system...'. Relevant

filing system means 'any set of information relating to individuals...
that specific information relating to a particular individual is readily
accessible...' Section 1 (1). However, following the decision of the Court
of Appeal in *Durrant* v. *Financial Services Authority* (2004), the Information
Commissioner has issued guidance on what constitutes a relevant filing
system, which is fairly restrictive, and means that some manual files may
not be covered. The Court of Appeal held that a 'relevant filing system'
should access data according to criteria about the subject, in a similar
way to a computer search. So a file on an employee would not be a 'relevant filing system' if the contents were just added randomly, or filed by
date order, so that a temp would have to leaf through the file to find the
relevant information. So the more disorganized the filing system, the
less likely it is to be covered!

Under section 7 of the DPA all 'data subjects' (in this case the
employee) have the right to request that 'data controllers' (ie the
company) communicate to them in intelligible form: i) the information
constituting any personal data of which that individual is the data
subject; and ii) any information available to the data controller as to
the source of those data (section 7 (c)). The request for access must be
made in writing (as has been done here) and the data controller may
ask for a processing fee of no more than £10. The disclosure must then
be made within the prescribed period of 40 days.

If the employee's file is computerized, or amounts to a 'relevant filing
system' (see above), then in terms of 'weeding out' the file the general
answer is that the DPA covers 'any' personal data and that it is only
permissible to withhold information if this is either expressly provided
for under the DPA or under general law. Under the latter category it
is likely that anything subject to genuine legal 'privilege' need not be
disclosed. This is a very limited category and would not cover these
internal memos. The only possible exception would be the right under
section 7 (4) and (5) to withhold information concerning a third party
(ie the manager) if that person's consent to the disclosure could not be
obtained. However, subsection 5 makes it clear that if consent cannot be
given then as much of the information as possible should be disclosed
whilst protecting the identity of the third party – this may mean blacking
out the name of the manager who wrote the note whilst disclosing
the content. Of course, should the employee issue court or tribunal
proceedings then the whole file (other than privileged material) is
likely to be disclosable in any event.

This emphasizes the fact that all data held concerning employees
should be as fair, relevant, accurate and up to date as possible. These
factors are all part of the principles of the DPA as set out in schedule

1 to that Act. If you would not be happy to stand by any information contained on an employee's file, and for that employee to see that information, then it should not be retained on the file.

See also page 174.

Chapter 7

Disciplinary

? Question

Annabelle has worked as a marketing assistant in the marketing department for three years. She has never been a great performer and almost failed her probationary period; however, with some coaching she seemed to improve, but now there are ongoing problems with her performance. Her managers find it frustrating that she has to be told things several times and mistakes are repeated. She has been inaccurate in her calculations in some proposals, which has cost the company money. She has not really been properly managed, and these deficiencies in performance have not been addressed in a consistent and coherent way.

A new manager, Brian, takes over the department. Brian is not that experienced, but he is enthusiastic and wants to see quick results. He feels that Annabelle has been given too easy a ride over the last three years, and he carries out a review of her work. He then conducts a meeting with Annabelle. Whilst Brian is professional throughout and raises legitimate concerns with Annabelle's work in a proper manner, she is taken aback by this new approach. After a couple of days she raises a grievance, claiming that Brian is bullying her. Brian is thrown off balance by this allegation and is now saying that he will not see through the points arising out of Annabelle's review, as he does not want to be labelled as a bully.

How do you resolve this situation?

Solution

This is an example of a phenomenon that can be described as 'reverse bullying'. A manager carries out a legitimate and proper performance improvement exercise, only to be met by an allegation of bullying on the part of the employee. It is quite possible for an employee to bully upwards as well as downwards, and arguably by raising a questionable allegation of bullying, it is the subordinate employee in fact doing the bullying.

Naturally a valid allegation of bullying has to be investigated carefully and taken seriously. As well as the obvious problems with staff morale and productivity, bullying could result in a constructive dismissal claim and, in a serious case, damages for psychiatric injury. The latter would be a personal injury claim which is likely to be covered by the organization's liability insurers, but nonetheless is obviously not a claim that any organization wants to have on its record.

Annabelle has raised a formal grievance and the statutory disciplinary and grievance procedures apply; therefore it is essential that the grievance is dealt with formally through the grievance procedure. On the facts as they are known, we believe it is unlikely that the grievance would be upheld. Provided it is done properly, pulling an employee up on deficient performance is not bullying.

The preferred sequence of events would be to hear the grievance and eliminate this allegation, so that Brian feels confident that he is not being regarded as a bully, and he should then be urged to return to see through the process that he has started.

You should ensure that there are clear, specific, fair and appropriate measurements put in place to monitor Annabelle's performance. Having such measurements is an effective way to defuse an allegation that performance improvement procedures are bullying. Ensure that the employee buys into the measurements at the outset, so that he or she cannot later claim that the measurements were unreasonable.

It may also be appropriate (probably in a more serious case) to bring in another person to work with Brian to ensure that his reviews are fair. That has to be handled with caution, as you do not wish to be seen to be undermining Brian or lending inadvertent credence to the allegation of bullying against him.

If Annabelle's performance does not improve, then the organization could move towards the more formal disciplinary process, which could potentially ultimately result in a dismissal on the grounds of capability.

Question

Bill the butcher has worked for the company for two years. Recently you dismissed Bill because it was found that he had stolen an item from the store. The item was found in his locker. Bill alleged that another employee had planted the item in his locker and, when spoken to, denied that he was guilty of theft or of any kind of misconduct.

You decided that Bill's allegation had no basis, and you thought that it was fanciful on his part that anyone would want to 'frame' him. You did not interview his co-workers, nor conduct a full interview with Bill. You proceeded to a disciplinary meeting at which Bill was dismissed. Bill is now alleging that you did not investigate the matter properly and that he was unfairly dismissed.

Was the investigation fair and reasonable in the circumstances? What constitutes an adequate investigation?

Solution

When the dismissal procedure began you were aware from the outset that this was a serious issue that could result in Bill being dismissed. The investigation that takes place as part of the disciplinary procedure is key to the final outcome. A careless procedure may mean that the disciplinary sanction is unfair.

Bill has stated that he believed another employee planted the item in his locker. You have dismissed this allegation as not being a possibility but you have taken this action without looking into it in any detail. You have not interviewed any other employees and you have not allowed Bill the opportunity to have his say.

Did anyone else have access to the lockers? Had Bill's keys gone missing? Had the locker been broken into? Did any of the other employees have a grudge against Bill?

A Tribunal is unlikely to find that it was the action of a reasonable employer to ignore relevant evidence, in particular where the employee was at risk of dismissal. In the circumstances the Tribunal is likely to find that you have acted unreasonably in not completing a full and fair investigation into the situation and that Bill was therefore unfairly dismissed.

So what will constitute a fair and reasonable investigation?

It is important to ensure that, in any case of alleged breach of the rules, the issue is properly investigated. The degree of the investigation will depend on the seriousness of the alleged breach and there should be no delay in carrying out the investigation. It is important that the person that investigates the matter establishes the facts. This may mean that witnesses will need to be interviewed. The purpose of carrying out the investigation is to help the employer determine whether the misconduct has occurred. Relevant information should never be ignored as it was in Bill's case.

Once the employer has made the proper enquiries, it is important to allow the employee to be able to respond to the allegation either by way of explanation or by way of mitigation.

It is necessary in accordance with the Employment Act 2002 (Dispute Resolution) Regulations 2004 to have a hearing before any decision is made as to whether to dismiss. The employee may be allowed to give an explanation during the investigative stage but, obviously, there is a risk that not all matters will have been put to the employee where, for instance, the investigation has not been completed. Ensure that at least one meeting with the employee takes place before dismissal or disciplinary action is taken.

You should have a clear written procedure for carrying out investigations and keep to it. Failing that, you should ensure you do the following:

1. Establish what the issue is.
2. Interview all relevant witnesses and keep written records.
3. Interview the accused employee and keep a written record.
4. Consider any issues raised by the witnesses or the employee that need to be looked into further.
5. Double-check any inconsistent points with the witnesses and the employee. Keep a written record.
6. Consider the evidence put forward by each person and decide how reliable the evidence is and how trustworthy the witnesses are; do any of them have a grudge against the accused or any reason to tell anything but the truth?
7. Allow the employee to see exactly what is being alleged and to respond to the allegations and points raised by the witnesses. Keep a written record.
8. You must take as much care with the investigation as the dismissal, as it forms part of the fairness of the decision.

The test that the Tribunal will apply is the objective standard of what the reasonable employer would do in the same circumstances. Keep this in mind when undertaking any investigation but in particular when there is a risk that the employee may be dismissed.

However, it is worth noting that the Employment Rights Act 1996, s. 98A(2) provides that where the employer has followed the minimum statutory disciplinary procedure, then failure to follow further procedural safeguards will not make the dismissal unfair by itself, as long as the employer can show that it would have decided to dismiss the employee even if it had followed the procedure. But this is unlikely to be the case here.

? Question

An office outing to France ends up with two senior managers drinking too much, starting an argument and having a punch-up on board Eurostar. It was over the weekend and seems to have been over something trivial, but a lot of bad feeling has been generated, with everyone taking sides.

What should you do?

Solution

It is rarely considered 'fair' to dismiss an employee for his or her conduct outside the workplace. The ACAS Code of Practice on Disciplinary & Grievance Procedures goes further still and states: 'If an employee is charged with, or convicted of, a criminal offence not related to work, this is not in itself reason for disciplinary action.'

However, although this fight took place outside the workplace, it was still 'connected to work' in that it took place during an office outing. You are vicariously liable for the actions of your employees during office outings (if, for example, the fight had been over racist comments that one party had made to the other, the aggrieved party would have been able to bring a harassment claim against the organization – *Chief Constable of the Lincolnshire Police* v. *Stubbs* (1999)) and therefore it would be perfectly fair to discipline both parties for their conduct. Putting both parties through a disciplinary procedure would hopefully also have the effect of subduing the 'side taking' among other employees – they would see that the organization is taking action and that a fair hearing is being given to both parties.

You may have a problem finding independent managers to chair the disciplinary hearings and appeal meetings, since the two people involved are both senior managers themselves. One answer might be to bring in an external chairman (perhaps a retired senior HR person) to hear the first-stage disciplinaries (this might also have the advantage of distancing the matter from the management team) and leaving the most senior manager in the organization free to hear any appeals.

Depending on the surrounding circumstances, it would not be outside the band of reasonable responses to dismiss both managers, if that is what the organization wants to do. Fighting and drunkenness are generally considered gross misconduct in most disciplinary procedures. However, you should treat both managers equally; it would be a mistake to use this as an excuse to get rid of one of the managers and keep the other one, unless the circumstances permit this.

There are some extenuating circumstances here, though (such as the fact that the organization presumably condoned some drinking during the office outing and the fact that the fight doesn't seem to have been too serious), and a warning of some kind for both participants would also be a reasonable response. This could be followed up with a general reminder to all staff of the organization's drug and alcohol policy.

? Question

Karen has been working for your company for eight years. Throughout the eight years you have experienced problems with Karen and the way she interacts with other employees in the office.

Karen will often refuse to speak to her colleagues and blame them for problems that she has caused herself. She has been known in the past to have threatened and intimidated a number of her colleagues.

Recently Karen has particularly upset one of her colleagues, Phoebe, through petty acts such as making drinks for everybody else on the table except her and being rude and abrupt to her when she asks Karen a question. Karen has not explained the reason for this to Phoebe.

You have a thick file on Karen that has built up over the years, full of complaints from other employees, including supervisors and managers. Recently, you have received two complaints from managers in relation to Karen's attitude to other members of staff and the upset she has been causing, and an e-mail from one of Karen's colleagues which concludes by saying 'I can't work with Karen any longer, her petty behaviour is making my work life unbearable, I am going to have to leave'.

1. What action should you take in this case?
2. Describe an 'ideal' disciplinary procedure – ie who should be the 'prosecutor' and 'judge'?

Solution

1. Karen has been performing adequately but the poor relationships that are being created within the workplace are leading to bad feelings and a great deal of upset. Action now needs to be taken in relation to Karen.

    The personality differences in the office are making the working environment unbearable for some members of staff. This is not simply a case of Karen not being able to get on with her employer but with all of her colleagues. You may potentially fairly dismiss

Karen on the grounds of either 'conduct' as Karen has threatened other members of staff, or 'some other substantial reason' as there appears to have been an irretrievable breakdown in the relationships between Karen and her colleagues.

In the case of *Treganowan* v. *Robert Knee & Co Ltd* (1975), T worked in an office with a number of other girls. The atmosphere in the office had become so tense that it was unbearable and was seriously affecting the company's business. The cause of the trouble was a personality clash between T and the other employees for which T was to blame. The hostility arose 'from a difference of opinion as to the merits of the permissive society' and T was 'completely insensitive to the atmosphere. T already had an illegitimate child and now she was boasting of her association with a boy almost half her age'. The Tribunal held that this constituted 'some other substantial reason' and that the dismissal was fair.

More recently, in *Perkins* v. *St George's Healthcare NHS Trust* (2005) the Court of Appeal held that although 'personality' itself cannot be a fair ground for dismissal, the way an employee's personality manifests itself may lead to dismissal for 'conduct' or 'some other substantial reason'.

You should consider carrying out a thorough investigation into the most recent complaints, interviewing as many of Karen's colleagues as possible, in particular those who have raised and been affected by the most recent complaints. It may be appropriate to suspend Karen whilst the investigation is carried out (provided you have the contractual right to do so), particularly when bearing in mind the previous threats that have been made by Karen and her intimidating behaviour towards colleagues. Once the investigation has been completed, the company's normal disciplinary procedure should be followed.

2. The 'ideal' disciplinary process should be as fair and be seen to be as fair as possible. From the company's perspective it is most important that roles are kept as distinct as possible. Without taking the analogy too far, it may be useful to picture a Magistrates Court: the Crown Prosecution Service presents the evidence for the prosecution, the defendant has an opportunity to answer the case and put forward his or her own evidence and the magistrates then make up their mind. Clearly in this case the magistrates are not involved in gathering the evidence against the defendant, nor are they involved in presenting the prosecution's case – imagine the uproar if they were!

Equally, a company must ensure that the person who chairs a disciplinary hearing is seen as independent and untainted by the investigation process. See the diagram in Figure 7.1.

As you can see, it may be necessary for HR to be involved as prosecutor and as advisor to the 'judge'. However, this should only be the case where there are sufficient people within HR for this to happen fairly. If the HR function is limited then it may be more appropriate for a senior manager to be the 'prosecutor' whilst HR remains as independent adviser.

As well as having distinct roles it is important that the employee 'defendant' is informed of their right to be accompanied at the hearing and has sufficient knowledge of the case being brought against them that they are able to defend themselves. 'Hi-jacking' employees with new allegations or new evidence at a disciplinary hearing is likely to lead to a finding of procedural unfairness.

? Question

One of your employees has been arrested and charged with being drunk on an aircraft, hitting a fellow passenger and assaulting a member of the cabin crew. He is due to stand trial next month and is planning to plead guilty. His solicitor has written to you asking you to provide a character reference to be used in mitigation at his trial.

You are appalled by this employee's behaviour. You are also worried that, as yours is a fairly high-profile company and 'air-rage' is a favourite topic of the press, this case may bring some adverse publicity for your company. Far from providing a character reference, you would rather sack him.

What can you do?

Solution !

You are certainly not obliged to provide a character reference for this employee.

However, as far as disciplinary procedures go, the situation is very different from the situation where a crime has been committed in the workplace. Tribunals and courts have been critical in the past of employers who automatically dismiss their employees because of crimes they have committed outside the workplace.

The main guidance on dismissing employees for criminal charges or convictions outside their employment is found in the ACAS Code of Practice on Disciplinary & Grievance Procedures. This states: 'These

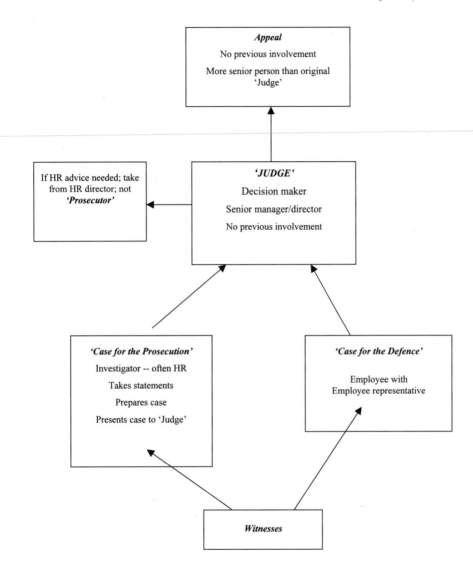

Figure 7.1 *Roles in a disciplinary hearing*

should not be treated as automatic reasons for dismissal. The main consideration should be whether the offence is one that makes workers unsuitable for their type of work.'

Case law suggests that worries over adverse publicity are insufficient grounds for dismissing an employee. While adverse publicity relating to this employee's court case would be unwelcome, it would be hard to prove that it would directly affect your business, for example in terms of sales.

Examples of cases where it has been successfully argued that a crime performed outside the workplace affected an employee's business interests include a shop security guard who was convicted of shoplifting and a railway worker who was convicted of assaulting a member of the British Transport Police.

If the employee is given a lengthy prison sentence, it could effectively 'frustrate' the contract of employment; that is, it will not be possible for him to carry out his side of the contract of employment and you can treat the contract as 'frustrated' – terminated by operation of law.

How 'lengthy' a prison sentence needs to be in order to frustrate a contract of employment is not entirely clear. The test is one of fact based on how long the employee is likely to be absent from work, whether you will have to engage a replacement and whether is it reasonable for you to engage a permanent rather than a temporary replacement.

Generally, sentences of 6 to 12 months have been held to be sufficiently 'lengthy' to frustrate contracts of employment. However, Tribunals are generally reluctant to hold that the contract has been 'frustrated', as this means they have no power to hear the case and assess reasonableness. You should be prepared to argue that though you have dismissed the employee, the dismissal was reasonable in all the circumstances of the case (the fact that he has been sentenced to a lengthy prison sentence).

In conclusion, unless this employee is convicted and handed a lengthy prison sentence, you would be well advised not to dismiss him because of this offence. Even if he is handed a prison sentence, you will be required to consider whether or not it would be possible to hold this employee's job open for him pending his return. However, you may want to consider disciplining this employee through the company's disciplinary procedure so that there is some record of this incident on his file.

The answer to this question may, however, be slightly different if the company has a contractual right to dismiss the employee for conduct which may 'bring the company into disrepute'. Whether or not the employee's actions in this case are capable of bringing the company into disrepute is a question of fact which may be affected by the seniority of the employee; for example, if it is the MD brawling on the aircraft then his name will be inextricably linked with the company's name, whereas if it is a very junior employee then the company's name may never be mentioned in connection with the matter. However, even if there is a contractual power to dismiss here, the dismissal can still be unreasonable under the law of unfair dismissal.

❓ Question

An Italian worker on an assembly line is repeatedly told by a fellow employee, who is English: 'I thought you Italians only ate pizzas.' The English employee is well known for his 'witty repartee' and makes comments of similar nature to many colleagues of various nationalities. He says this was harmless banter, taken in good spirit by everyone else, but the Italian employee has taken offence.

1. What should you do to address the situation?
2. What claims could the Italian bring and against whom?
3. What further should have been done to protect both the Italian employee and the company?

Solution ❗

1. First, there should be a thorough fact-finding investigation to ascertain the extent and seriousness of the English employee's comments in relation to all employees, including the Italian employee. If the fact-finding exercise concludes that the comments do not warrant more serious action or if the situation has not become irretrievable, would it be possible to 'mediate' between the two employees? If the fact finding suggests that more serious action should be taken then the English employee should be subject to disciplinary action and, potentially, dismissal.

    The Italian employee may also wish to use the grievance procedure to give full vent to his concerns.

2. If the internal mechanisms do not succeed in defusing the situation then it is quite possible that the Italian employee could make a complaint under the Race Relations Act 1976 on the grounds that he has suffered a detriment on the grounds of his ethnic or national origin. This claim would be primarily against the company on the grounds that it is vicariously liable for the acts of the English employee committed in the course of his employment. Whether or not such acts were in the 'course of employment' is open to debate but the fact that they took place on the factory floor during working hours may make it difficult for the company to argue otherwise.

    The Italian employee could also join the English employee into the proceedings. The employee is usually named as an alternate respondent in such cases, partly as an insurance policy in case the employer succeeds in making out the 'employer's defence', see below.

The revised Race Relations Act (RRA) 1976 (Amendment) Regulations 2003 introduced separate free-standing provisions covering harassment at work, defined as unwanted conduct which takes place with the purpose or effect of undermining someone's dignity, or creating an intimidating, hostile, degrading, humiliating or offensive environment for the individual. However, this only covers harassment on grounds of nationality or colour, only 'race or ethnic or national origins'.

It may also be possible to bring an action against the employer using the Protection from Harassment Act (1997), following the decisions in *Majrowski* v. *Guy's and St Thomas's NHS Trust* (2005) and *Banks* v. *Ablex Ltd* (2005).

3. Under section 32 (3) RRA it is a defence against a claim for vicarious race discrimination if the employer can demonstrate 'that he took such steps as were reasonably practicable to prevent the employee from doing that act'.

So what steps could the company have taken to prevent the English employee making these comments?

1. Have in place a clear and unambiguous Equal Opportunities Policy making it clear that racially motivated language is not acceptable.
2. Ensure that this policy is available to, and is promulgated to, the workforce (perhaps through training).
3. Enforce the policy. If the English employee was well known for his racially based 'witty repartee' then the company should have been disciplining him at a much earlier stage.

Employers should also be aware that harassment on grounds of sex, race, sexuality, disability and sexual orientation are all unlawful, with age scheduled to follow in October 2006. One person's idea of 'witty repartee' may be deeply offensive to others.

See also Chapter 1.

? Question

You are the HR director of a company which supplies and manages staff on various oil rigs and other offshore installations. You have been hearing rumours that some recent recruits are taking drugs on board the rigs and that this may have led to a 'near miss' safety incident.

Can you impose random drug testing on your employees and compulsory drug testing as part of your future recruitment policy? If so then, practically, how do you go about it?

Solution !

You cannot impose drug testing (random or otherwise) on employees without their consent. Even if the employee's contract or handbook contained a general statement that the company reserves the right to require employees to undergo random testing, each individual test could only be done with the employee's consent – there can be no enforced drug testing, nor can there be covert gathering of samples for testing.

Having said that, any drug testing policy should make it clear that a refusal to give consent to a drugs test (or of course a positive result) will lead to unpaid suspension and disciplinary action. If the company wishes to introduce a new policy then this would be best done by way of an amendment to a non-contractual section of a company handbook rather than seeking to impose this as a contractual change, which is a more complex process.

Any policy and disciplinary action should of course be proportionate to the perceived risk. In the example above, a random drug testing policy backed up by dismissal for gross misconduct may be reasonable on an oil rig owing to the very real safety issues. This may be less reasonable in an office environment or perhaps in an industry where recreational drug use is more acceptable (dare we say parts of the entertainment industry?).

In relation to testing all recruits, this is probably fine provided that everyone is tested in the same way and at the same stage of the process, to avoid any implications of discrimination arising.

To carry out effective testing you need to consider three types of test, depending on the circumstances. Snort cocaine, and it's in your brain in seven seconds. Minutes later it's in your oral fluid. In a matter of hours it's in your urine. A week or two later, it will be in hair cut from your scalp.

Shortly after a cocaine hit, a urine test would be negative, unless you were a habitual user. But an oral fluid test would be positive. Conversely, if your oral fluid was tested after a couple of days, it would be negative, even though a urine test would then be positive.

Many people abstain from drugs prior to a job interview. Hair testing is the only suitable technology to use here. But for random drug screening, urine tests are ideal. Each technology has its benefits, and

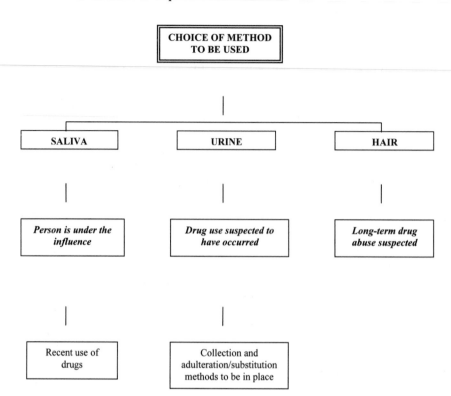

Figure 7.2   *Methods of drug testing*

each one has its place in your screening programme: saliva detects very recent drug use or impairment; urine detects drug use in the last few days; hair detects drug use in the last three months.

Question

Roger is a trainee in a law firm and his supervisory solicitor is Janet. Roger comes to see you because last night while he was working late he saw Janet photocopying documents and is sure that she does not need them for any client cases she is on.

He does not think Janet knew he was there and is too scared to give any evidence against her. You have already heard rumours that Janet is leaving the firm to work for a local competing law firm.

How can you convince Roger to help you investigate?

Solution ❗

In light of the rumours that you have heard about Janet, this will obviously raise suspicions as to why she should be photocopying any documents. If Janet is called to an investigatory meeting, then one of the first questions that she will probably ask is who saw her photocopying the documents. Roger has real concerns that if there is no substance to his allegations and Janet's actions were totally innocent, he will certainly not be Janet's favourite trainee solicitor and may suffer as a result of this. Although you will try to assure him as best you can that if nothing comes out of his allegations he will be protected from any bullying or harassment from Janet, and he can raise a grievance in that respect if it happens, this will not be an attractive offer to Roger who certainly does not want to get into such wrangles with the person who is his line manager.

It will therefore be possible to ask him to provide his version of events in an anonymous witness statement. If this is going to be done, it is essential that whether he has a grudge to bear against Janet is investigated. For example, has she given him a recent bad appraisal or just simply told him off for some poor work that he had undertaken?

You would also want to investigate whether his evidence can be corroborated and so you would need to find out whether there was anybody else in the office that evening who may have seen Janet or Roger. You would also be asking Roger why he was in the office late that evening and perhaps investigating exactly what work he was undertaking.

In these circumstances Janet would not need to know who saw her photocopying the documents and would hopefully not be able to guess who was giving that evidence against her. However, in some circumstances, giving anonymous witness evidence is not possible as the complainant will be central to the issue. For example, if an allegation of harassment is made against somebody, then the only way that person can defend the claim is by knowing whom he or she has allegedly harassed.

With regard to the actual witness statement, you would follow the guidelines given by the case of *Linfood Cash and Carry* v. *Thomson* (1989) and have Roger's evidence in a written statement, seeking corroboration and finding out whether Roger has a grudge to bear.

If there is a disciplinary hearing in respect of these allegations and Janet raises issues which need to be put to Roger, then the chairman/decision maker should adjourn the disciplinary hearing and speak to Roger, putting the questions to him that Janet has raised and making a decision from there.

Question

Michelle has broken her leg and has been off sick for three weeks. You happen to be at her desk whilst talking to a colleague and look in her desk drawer for a stapler. On lifting up some papers you discover a small envelope, which you open to find some pre-rolled cigarettes. They look like cannabis joints.

Can you take any action even though Michelle is signed off sick?

Solution

If the pre-rolled cigarettes are cannabis joints, then possession of these is illegal and disciplinary action could be taken against Michelle. The extent of the disciplinary action does depend on how any previous drug-related issues have been dealt with and also whether the company has a drugs policy and what the drugs policy says. Possession of such drugs could be considered an act of gross misconduct and therefore could lead to Michelle's dismissal.

There would, of course, still need to be an investigatory as well as a disciplinary hearing as, for example, you may find that the cigarettes do in fact just contain tobacco, or Michelle may have some mitigating explanation, for example that they actually belong to somebody else in the department who stores them in her desk drawer.

Before you even get to this stage, however, you need to ascertain whether you can take any action. This depends largely on whether you should have been in Michelle's drawer without her permission. Will she claim, if any action is taken against her, that this was a breach of one of her human rights, that being Article 8 which is the right to respect for private and family life, home and correspondence? This depends largely on whether or not Michelle could have had a reasonable expectation of privacy in respect of her desk drawer. Could it be considered general practice that the desk drawers are used solely for company stationery and that no one else thinks that private belongings can be kept in those drawers? Do employees have their own keys to their drawers, which can be locked in their absence? All such factors would need to be considered in regard to whether or not you should have had access to her desk drawer.

If a Tribunal agreed that the right to privacy was breached, it would effectively strike out the employer's case, since all evidence is based on the Human Rights Act (HRA) breach. However, in this situation it is unlikely – the opening of the drawer was not an intrusive invasion of privacy.

Assuming that you do decide to take such action, then you should make a file note or a statement immediately, advise Michelle's line manager of the circumstances and take the pre-rolled cigarettes/joints out of the desk drawer, keeping them somewhere safe. On Michelle's return she should be called in to a meeting with yourself and the line manager and the circumstances should be explained to her. At this stage the disciplinary process will be followed as usual.

? Question

Craig is one of the best salesmen that the company has. Recently he has been returning from his lunch breaks smelling of alcohol. His line manager has spoken to him and Craig has laughed off the issue, saying he likes the odd pint or so. His work has started to deteriorate but he still achieves above-average targets. His line manager seeks your advice on how to handle the situation.

How do you respond?

Solution

How you handle this situation is dependent on whether or not you have a policy on alcohol use and what it says. If employers do not have a policy on alcohol and drugs use then it certainly is one that should be introduced. Alcohol and drugs policies should state exactly what is not permitted and this would cover whether drinking during any lunch or rest breaks is permitted. Therefore, in these circumstances, Craig would be in breach of the policy and could be told that disciplinary action will be taken against him. If in these circumstances Craig is denying that he has been drinking or is denying that he has had as much alcohol as you think he has, then a policy which allows random alcohol or drug testing (which would usually be permitted only in reasonable circumstances) would allow you to ask him to be tested. Again, if he refused and this was something contained in the employer's policy then it would be a breach of the policy and disciplinary action could be taken accordingly.

Without such a policy it may still be reasonable if you ask Craig to undertake a random alcohol test, as he seems to be drinking regularly and this is affecting his work and has caused concern to his line manager. If he refused then it could be considered a refusal to carry out a reasonable instruction and disciplinary action could be taken.

However, you should also consider whether such a request could be seen as an invasion of Craig's privacy, rights which now have some protection under the Human Rights Act 1998. Obviously if he did agree to take an alcohol test after returning from one of his lunches and it is found that he has a very small amount of alcohol in his bloodstream then it would be difficult to take any action. However, bringing the issue to his attention would mean that any further instances of alcohol abuse could be dealt with in a harsher manner as he has been put on warning that the issue has been brought to your attention already.

At the same time, Craig is obviously a very productive worker and you do not wish to see him being dismissed or resigning because of this. Therefore, if you are concerned that he has an alcohol problem, recommending he see his GP or your occupational health services in order to undertake some counselling or even trying to arrange that counselling for him could be the best way forward.

Question

You are currently engaged in a difficult disciplinary investigation and the employee involved has written to you saying that he intends to tape record the forthcoming disciplinary meeting. Are you obliged to agree to that? What are the implications if either party secretly tape records the meeting?

Solution

Subject to anything about tape recording appearing in the disciplinary procedure, which is unlikely, there is no legal obligation on an employer to permit an employee to tape a meeting. You can therefore refuse the request and point out to the employee (which will presumably be the case) that someone will be in attendance to take comprehensive written notes that will later be typed. On the other hand, if it is a complicated and difficult disciplinary, is there any real reason for declining the request to tape the meeting? After all you should conduct the meeting correctly in accordance with your own procedures and any ACAS guidelines, and you should have nothing to hide. Sometimes arguments about this issue can detract from the real substance of the matter, so in many instances it might be a pragmatic approach to agree to the recording. If you disagree with any transcript further down the line, you can ask to hear the recording; ensure that you receive an undertaking from the employee not to delete the recording.

Either party secretly tape recording the meeting can be a contentious situation. These days the technology for hidden recording equipment is readily available, so from a technical point of view it is easy to do.

Although people are prone to say that secret tape recordings cannot be used in Court, in fact there is no such strict rule in Employment Tribunals. A Chairman can exercise his discretion to listen to the tape or read a transcript if he thinks that the hearing of the case will be enhanced.

If the employer tapes the meeting secretly the employee might make a complaint to the Information Commissioner alleging a breach of one or more of the data protection principles. There is as yet no clear determination on this issue as to whether or not it would indeed be regarded as a breach of the Data Protection Act.

An employee is also likely to argue that Article 8 of the Human Rights Act, the Right to Respect for Private and Family Life, has been encroached. If a Tribunal or other court agreed, it could disallow any evidence in the case based on or obtained through a breach of human rights. This therefore has significance potentially for both public and private sector employers (the Human Rights Act not having direct application to the latter). Again, an undecided point on which the outcome would depend on a detailed analysis of all the circumstances.

Given however that there is a possibility of complaint and/or legal action by the employee if the employer secretly tapes, there is no point in doing so, just to create a problem. If you have a reason to tape the meeting, then do so openly. The employee certainly has no right to object to that.

In a recent case an employee secretly taped the disciplinary hearings, including some of the private deliberations of the panel. The issue of the admissibility of that evidence went to the Employment Appeal Tribunal. The EAT allowed the secret recording of the disciplinary hearings to be used, but not the recording of the private deliberations of the panel.

See also page 87.

❓ Question

Sally is an accounts clerk. Thursday was Sally's birthday and some of her colleagues met up with her during the evening at a local pub to celebrate. Although most of them left early, Sally stayed on with some other friends and, it appears, carried on drinking late into the night. On Friday, Sally turned up at work clearly the worse for wear and smelling strongly of alcohol. Her line manager wants to dismiss her on the grounds of gross misconduct.

Can he?

Solution !

It is well established that for a dismissal to be fair, the employee must have been warned that his or her job is in jeopardy. If a ■ disciplinary rule states that particular breaches will be considered gross misconduct and will attract instant dismissal, then that will constitute a warning.

Even if your procedure lists 'drunkenness' as an example of gross misconduct, Sally could (as many employees have in the past!) argue that she was not 'drunk' and that therefore she was never warned that coming to work slightly hungover from the night before would be a dismissible offence.

It is also important to consider how similar cases have been treated in the past. If such behaviour has been tolerated before, or has led to less severe sanctions, such as written warnings, than it is unlikely to be fair to dismiss Sally. If the employer wants to change the policy concerning such matters, it should state so clearly, explain that although such behaviour has been tolerated in the past, this will no longer be the case, and spell out the likely consequences.

You could try to argue that the rule was so obvious that it was implied in her contract of employment. However, in the case of *Meyer Dunmer International Limited* v. *Rogers* (1978), the Employment Appeal Tribunal (EAT) said that, if an employer wants to rely on a rule to justify dismissal for a first offence, the rule must be plainly adopted, plainly and clearly set out and great publicity must be given to it so that every employee knows beyond doubt that if he or she breaches the rule, he or she will be dismissed.

If your intention is actually to have a zero-tolerance policy on alcohol, it would be a good idea to change your policy to reflect that. The phrase 'under the influence of alcohol' is less ambiguous than 'drunkenness'.

? Question

A customer has made a complaint about Bob, one of your ■ receptionists. She says Bob was extremely rude to her mentally disabled son. Bob has seen the letter and categorically denies the allegation. No one else witnessed the alleged incident. Because of the seriousness of the allegation, Bob's manager has decided to escalate the matter to a disciplinary. Bob says the only way to deal with the matter in a disciplinary hearing is to invite the accuser to the meeting so that he can cross-examine her on her letter.

Do you have to allow this?

Solution

Natural justice seems to suggest that employees who are accused of misconduct should be allowed to challenge their accusers and test the evidence against them. Certainly, were Bob accused of such conduct in a criminal court or even in a civil court, he would be offered the opportunity to do so.

However, criminal courts have to prove guilt 'beyond all reasonable doubt'. Civil courts have to prove guilt 'on the balance of probabilities'. Disciplinary procedures do not have to prove guilt at all – they merely have to lead to the decision maker genuinely believing (based on reasonable investigation) that the person is guilty. For this reason, Tribunals have accepted that there is no requirement on employers to allow employees to cross-examine their accusers.

In the case of *Santamera* v. *Express Cargo Forwarding* (2003), the EAT held that an accused employee did not have to be given the right or the opportunity to cross-examine her accusers, and went on to say: 'The employer has to act fairly, but fairness does not require a forensic or quasi-judicial investigation, for which the employer is in any event unlikely to be qualified and for which it may lack the means.'

Of course, there may be situations where it would be impossible to act fairly without allowing cross-examination of a particular witness, but those cases will be the exception.

In this case, you should ask the customer if she is prepared to attend a disciplinary hearing. If she refuses, you should consider her reason for refusing in weighing up the evidence against Bob.

Question

Your company provides IT services within schools. Dave, one of your IT consultants, works in three local senior schools. You have just learnt that he has been arrested and charged with having several images of child pornography on his home computer. The case has not yet gone to court and you understand it could be several months before it does so. In the meantime, he has been released on bail.

You are obviously very concerned about what will happen if Dave continues visiting the schools and the parents or teachers find out. What do you do?

Solution ▋

It is rarely considered 'fair' to dismiss an employee for his or her criminal conduct outside the workplace. The ACAS Code of Practice on Disciplinary & Grievance Procedures goes further still and states: 'If an employee is charged with, or convicted of, a criminal offence not related to work, this is not in itself reason for disciplinary action.'

However, in this case, the conduct that the person has been charged with is related to his work. He works with children and he has been charged with a sexual offence involving children.

You have been told that it could be 'several months' before the case goes to court. In that time, it will be extremely difficult for you to justify sending Dave to work in schools. However, Tribunals have deemed it unfair to dismiss employees on the grounds that they have been charged with a criminal offence. In the case of *Securicor Guarding Ltd* v. *R* (1994), R was a security guard who was arrested and charged with sex offences against children. His employer asked him about the offences and he denied them. However, the employer dismissed him because of the impossible situation that it believed it would be put in if it did not dismiss him. The EAT held: 'The mere fact that an employee in a sensitive position has been charged with an offence will not justify the employer in dismissing him, rather than suspending him or moving him away from the sensitive position until the truth of the matter is determined.'

Employers must also avoid an immediate 'knee-jerk' reaction in cases like this. In *Gogay* v. *Hertfordshire County Council* (2000), the council suspended a care worker, following an allegation of sexual abuse. This was held to be a breach of mutual trust and confidence, as it should have considered other options, such as a transfer, or period of leave. The employee suffered psychological injuries as a result of the suspension, and was awarded over £26,000 in damages.

If possible, look into the possibility of Dave taking on another role on a temporary basis until the truth is known.

As for investigating the matter yourself, Dave is under no obligation to help you; the police may pass on a certain amount of information but this is unlikely to be enough to allow you to carry out a 'reasonable investigation' of your own into the question of whether Dave really is guilty of holding images of child pornography on his home computer.

If you are seriously considering dismissing Dave now, then at the very least you must follow the statutory Disciplinary and Dismissal Procedure (DDP) and make sure Dave has a chance to put his case. The standard of proof is not so high in disciplinary procedures as it is in criminal proceedings, and you do not have to be satisfied beyond all reasonable doubt that Dave is guilty of the charge in order for the dismissal to be fair.

Question

You employ Bob, a maintenance man. Two years ago, while fixing a boiler, he left a live electric cable hanging over the sink in the open office kitchen. Fortunately the next person in the kitchen noticed the cable and sorted the problem out. Bob was given a formal written warning (to stay on his file for 12 months) and told that if he did anything like that again he would be dismissed. Last week, while servicing the boiler, he did exactly the same thing again.

What can you do?

Solution

The obvious answer would seem to be to dismiss him on the grounds of capability. He's been warned he would be dismissed if it happened again and the act could potentially have had dire consequences.

However, the warning was given to him two years ago and has expired. It is well established that expired warnings cannot be taken into account when disciplining employees but this was taken to a surprising length in the recent case of *Diosynth Ltd* v. *Thomson* (2006).

In this case, the Court of Session considered the dismissal of an employee (Mr Thomson) who worked on a chemical plant. Mr Thomson failed to carry out an important health and safety measure (inerting a vessel) and as a result there was a methanol leakage and an explosion which caused the death of a colleague.

It turned out that Mr Thomson had failed to inert a vessel some 18 months before and had been given a warning. He had promised he would always do so in future. The warning had lasted 12 months, and expired 5 months before the fatal incident. Mr Thomson was dismissed and the person hearing the disciplinary said he had concluded Mr Thomson was incapable of following clear warnings.

Mr Thomson brought a claim of unfair dismissal. He was unsuccessful in the Employment Tribunal but the case was appealed all the way to the Court of Session, which ruled in his favour.

The lessons to be learnt from this case are: 1) a reminder that expired warnings cannot – even in the most extreme of circumstances – be taken into account in disciplinary hearings; 2) for the most serious acts, you should consider issuing warnings without time limits. This runs counter to the ACAS Guidelines (and may be out of line with most disciplinary policies) but the Court of Session suggested warnings could be issued without time limits.

It is extremely difficult to dismiss employees fairly for single acts of incapability. Proving that an employee has been guilty of 'gross incompetence' generally requires evidence that their act could have had 'calamitous consequences' or evidence of 'irredeemable incapability' – a high burden that cannot normally be reached.

In this case, if you are going to dismiss, it would be safer to rely on the one act and try to pin the dismissal on 'gross incapability' than it would to rely on the previous, expired warning.

? Question

One of your employees, Mike, was photographed by another employee, Paul, whilst he was allegedly asleep on duty. Mike claims he was on a rest break and was therefore entitled to sleep if he wished. Neither of the employees is well known for being truthful.

You want to dismiss, but should you?

Solution

There are six potentially fair reasons to dismiss an employee; they are capability, redundancy, some other substantial reason, breach of an enactment, conduct and retirement. Clearly the most relevant reason for dismissal in this instance is conduct, in that the employee was allegedly asleep when he should have been working.

The difficulty is that an employee whom you know to be not particularly trustworthy has made the allegation. What do you do next?

Investigation

A thorough investigation should be undertaken to establish whether there were any other witnesses and also to take full statements from both Mike and Paul. Does Mike have a reasonable explanation? Is it possible that he is telling the truth? Does Paul have a grudge against Mike? Is there any reason he is not telling the truth?

Once the investigation has been completed, what is the next step?

Consider the evidence

What do the statements say? What other evidence has been found? Is there enough evidence now to move forward to a disciplinary hearing?

If the answer is no, Mike should be advised that no further action will be taken. It is also worth emphasizing that sleeping on duty is considered by the company to be unacceptable behaviour and where proven would lead to disciplinary action.

Disciplinary

If there is enough evidence to move to a disciplinary hearing, a 'Step 1' letter should be sent to Mike advising him of the allegations, when and where the hearing will be, and that he has the right to be accompanied by a colleague or trade union representative. All of the relevant evidence that has been collected from the investigation should also be sent to Mike along with the Step 1 letter.

The disciplinary hearing should then be held at which Mike should be given every opportunity to state his case. Following the disciplinary Mike should be advised of his right to appeal any disciplinary decision that is taken.

Once Mike has been advised of your decision, if he disagrees with it, he should send you his written appeal. Once you have received this you should write to Mike confirming the date/time/place of the appeal hearing and again confirm his right to be accompanied by a colleague or trade union representative.

What if, following the disciplinary, the evidence is inconclusive?

Making a disciplinary decision based on inconclusive evidence will always be difficult. In this situation a warning will be the most appropriate sanction, because although there is photographic evidence, it is impossible to be sure when the photograph was taken and neither Mike nor Paul is a trustworthy character. A dismissal in this situation is likely to be an unreasonable sanction.

Chapter 8

Parental rights

? Question

You have noticed that one of your line managers, David, has been taking a lot of time off recently to care for his wife. Most of this leave has been taken as paid holiday, but he has also asked for, and been granted, some unpaid leave.

Each time David takes some leave he seems to extend it and isn't keeping the company fully informed of the reason for his absence and his likely return date. This has got worse over the past couple of months and is causing discontent amongst the other line managers who are starting to wonder whether the reasons given by David for the leave are genuine.

Is David entitled to the leave? If so, are you able to restrict the amount of leave that is taken? Are you able to force David to keep the company informed about the reason for and length of his absence?

Solution !

Under the Employment Rights Act 1996 (ERA) all employees are entitled to time off to care for dependants. The circumstances in which an employee is able to take such time off are outlined in s57A of the Employment Rights Act (ERA); these are as follows:

(a) to provide assistance on an occasion when a dependant falls ill, gives birth or is injured or assaulted,

(b) to make arrangements for the provision of care for a dependant who is ill or injured,

(c)   in consequence of the death of a dependant,

(d)   because of the unexpected disruption or termination of arrange-
      ments for the care of a dependant, or

(e)   to deal with an incident involving a child of the employee which
      occurs unexpectedly in a period during which an educational
      establishment is responsible for the child.

Clearly, David's reason, if genuine, will fall within (a) above. However, the right to take leave to care for dependants is a right to 'reasonable time off' during the employee's working hours in order to take 'action which is necessary'.

The case of *Qua* v. *John Ford Morrison Solicitors* (2003) interpreted the provisions as meaning that the right existed in respect of 'unexpected or sudden events affecting their dependants' and to make 'any necessary longer term arrangements for their care'. If David's wife has a long-term illness, it is unlikely that he will fall within the circumstances for him to qualify for the leave. This will therefore need to be investigated further.

There is nothing in the statute which would require David to produce evidence for the reason for the leave; however, if you are concerned that David is abusing the right to time off you should deal with the situation in accordance with your normal disciplinary procedures. You should request that David produce evidence to support the explanation that he has given for the leave and, if necessary, to prove his relationship with the person affected by the illness. Assuming that you have then established that the reason for the leave taken is genuine, you are still concerned by the amount of leave that is being taken.

Unfortunately, there is no formal limit on the number of occasions on which time can be taken off to care for dependants. On each occasion you will need to consider whether the request falls within the categories specified at (a)–(e) above and if so whether the situation is 'unexpected' or 'sudden', requiring the employee to take time off from work.

You are able to refuse to permit David to take the time off, but only in circumstances in which it is reasonable. There are two main grounds on which leave may be refused: 1) where it is not necessary for the employee to take time off work; 2) where the amount of time requested off work by the employee is unreasonable.

The disruption or inconvenience caused to the company is an irrele-vant factor and should not be taken into account when considering refusing leave. If you unreasonably refuse time off, the employee will be able to make a complaint to the Employment Tribunals. Female employees may also have a claim for indirect sex discrimination.

What about keeping the company informed of his likely absence? In accordance with the relevant rules, David must comply with certain notice provisions. He must tell the company the reason for his absence as soon as reasonably practicable, and how long he expects to be absent.

If David fails to comply with these notice requirements, he will lose the right to time off. You will then be able to treat David in the same way as you would treat any employee on unauthorized leave and instigate the disciplinary procedure.

You must ensure that you act reasonably and bear in mind that it may not be reasonably practicable for David to inform you of the reason for his leave until his return, although this is likely to apply only in exceptional circumstances. Always investigate thoroughly before taking any disciplinary action!

Note also that the right to request flexible working patterns, currently only available to parents with children under six years old, is to be extended to those caring for adults by the Work and Families Bill 2006.

Question

You employ a senior sales executive, Jean, to cover the North of England. Jean has worked for you for two years. Jean's role requires her to be available five days a week and to divide her time between the office and customers' business premises. You have received a flexible working request from Jean, but think it unlikely that you will be able to agree to her request, which would mean reducing her hours to just three days per week to enable her to care for her young child.

What issues should you take into account in deciding whether or not the request should be granted?

Solution

There are two issues to be considered here: the right to request flexible working, and indirect sex discrimination.

The right of employees to request flexible working places a duty on employers to consider all applications and establish whether the desired work pattern can be accommodated within the needs of the business.

Jean is an employee and has been with the company for at least 26 weeks. We also know that Jean is the mother to a child under the age of six for whom she is responsible and that she is making this application to enable her to care for that child. Therefore Jean fits within the eligibility criteria to enable her to make a flexible working request.

For Jean's application to be valid it must:

- be in writing;
- state that the application is being made under the statutory right to request a flexible working pattern;
- confirm the employee has responsibility for the upbringing of the child and is either:
  - the mother, father, adopter, guardian or foster parent; or
  - married to the partner of the child's mother, father, adopter, guardian or foster parent;
- explain what effect, if any, the employee thinks the proposed change would have on the employer and how, in their opinion, any such effect may be dealt with;
- specify the flexible working pattern applied for;
- state the date on which it is proposed the change should become effective;
- state whether a previous application has been made to the employer and, if so, when it has been made;
- be dated.

Jean is requesting that her work pattern change from full-time hours of five days per week to part-time hours of three days per week.

There are specific business grounds upon which an application can be refused and it is these grounds that should be taken into account when considering whether or not it is possible for the company to accept the proposed change in the employee's working pattern. The business grounds for refusing a request are as follows:

1. burden of additional costs;
2. detrimental effect on ability to meet customer demand;
3. inability to reorganize work amongst existing staff;
4. inability to recruit additional staff;
5. detrimental impact on quality;
6. detrimental impact on performance;
7. insufficiency of work during the periods the employee proposes to work;
8. planned structural changes.

As part of Jean's application she should have stated what the impact of the proposed change would be on the company. The company in return should look at each point on the above list and consider the effect that the change in Jean's working pattern will have on the company, other employees, customers etc.

For example, will Jean be able to visit all of the customers necessary within three days instead of five days? If the answer is no, then the company will be able to rely on reason 2 in the above list and may also be able to rely on reasons 5 and 6.

If you decide to reject Jean's request, the explanation given for the rejection must be sufficient. It does not need to be particularly long or complex but should give full details. It should start with the ground relied upon, which should be specifically stated and followed by an explanation, with reasons, as to why that ground applies in this situation, for example:

> I am sorry that I cannot grant your request to reduce your hours of work from five days to three days per week, but this would have a detrimental effect on the ability to meet customer demands.
>
> It is necessary for you to work five days to ensure that you are able to visit all of our customers in the North of England on a weekly basis to ensure that purchasing requirements are met and that orders are processed by Friday lunchtime each week. If you were to reduce your hours to three days per week I do not believe that you would have sufficient time to enable you to comply with these requirements.

If an application is rejected you must write to Jean in the above terms and you must also ensure that the appeal procedure is set out and that the written notice has been dated.

Alternatively, if once having examined the business grounds and considered the request as a whole you come to the conclusion that Jean's application can be accepted, it must be accepted in the following written format. It must:

- detail the new work pattern,
- state the date on which it will start, and
- ensure that the notice is dated.

Once the request has been accepted, the change to Jean's working pattern will be permanent.

There are specific requirements in relation to the timing of meetings and notices that must be followed within the procedure to ensure that an application is dealt with in a timely manner. This timeline is detailed in the flow chart shown in Figure 8.1.

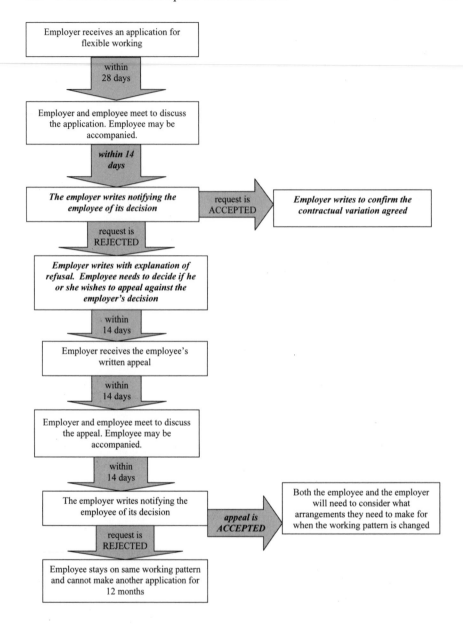

Figure 8.1   *Procedure on right to request a flexible working pattern*

However, even though it may be lawful to refuse Jean's request under the flexible working legislation, it may still be indirect sex discrimination not to allow her to move to three days a week. It is well established that a requirement for full-time working will disadvantage more women than men, as it is an accepted fact that women are the primary carers of small children. The key question then will be whether you can justify this requirement in Jean's case. You will need to produce evidence of why it is essential that Jean works full-time, and you need to undertake a balancing exercise between Jean's needs and your reasonable requirements, as Tribunals use a test of proportionality. In considering a sex discrimination claim in this context, the Tribunal will go much further in examining your business reasons than is the case where a flexible working application is under scrutiny.

? Question

A pregnant employee has nominated the first day of the week in which her baby is due as the start of her maternity leave. That is still four months away. She says she can no longer work the 'early' shift (0700–1500) or the 'late' shift (1300–2100) and just wants to work 'days' (0900–1700).

Is the employee entitled to nominate this day as the start of her maternity leave? Is the company obliged to agree to her request to work days only?

Solution !

An employee is entitled to nominate any date that she chooses as the first day of her maternity leave. It is perhaps unlikely that the maternity leave will, in this case, actually start on the nominated day. It is very late in the pregnancy and in practice maternity leave will start on the earliest of: the nominated date; childbirth; or the first absence wholly or partly by reason of pregnancy within the four weeks before the expected week of childbirth. An employee who is claiming, four months before the baby is due, that she cannot do this or that is perhaps not very likely to last the course during the last four weeks before the expected week of childbirth.

If her claim that she cannot work early and late shifts is valid, then she may be entitled to have her request just to work days granted. Under the relevant legislation, a pregnant employee who cannot perform her normal duties 'in consequence of any relevant requirement or relevant recommendation' is entitled, if there is alternative work on terms and conditions not substantially less favourable, to be offered that or, unless she unreasonably refuses such an offer, to be suspended on full pay. An important question here, therefore, is whether this employee's statement that she can no longer work early or late shifts arises under a relevant requirement or recommendation.

On the face of it, it does not. This is because the only express reference to hours of work in any such requirement or recommendation relates to 'night work'. Under reg.17 of the Management of Health and Safety at Work Regulations 1999, 'Where (a) a new or expectant mother works at night; and (b) a certificate from a registered medical practitioner or a registered midwife shows that it is necessary for her health or safety that she should not be at work for any period of such work identified in the certificate', an employer is under a specific duty to offer her alternative work (including changing her hours) or suspend her on pay. Here, however, work at night is not involved.

This does not mean that the employer can simply ignore, or refuse out of hand, the employee's request. An employer is under a duty to undertake and, if circumstances change, to keep updated a risk assessment in relation to all the working conditions – including hours – of a pregnant employee and the DTI's guidance says, 'If an individual believes there is a risk to her health or safety, or to that of her baby, which her employer has not considered in the risk assessment, she should bring the risk to the attention of her employer or health and safety representative.' This employee's approach might be viewed as doing just that. But simply saying that she cannot work the early and late shifts does not identify the health risk that doing so might involve.

The employer is entitled to ask for some medical justification for the employee's assertion that she cannot work at particular times and, at least in theory, if no such justification is provided, refuse her request just to work on days. In practice, the employer will need to be careful. If her request is refused but she then does not turn up for late or early shifts the employer will need to take action against her, and it is likely that she will argue that any such action was taken on grounds of her pregnancy and so amounts to direct sex discrimination. This does not mean that any such claim would necessarily succeed, but the employer will need to be sure that any action that it takes could stand up to such a challenge.

If there are any shift premia involved in the early and late shifts they will probably need to be maintained if the employee is moved onto days. This is because it has been held that the provision of terms 'not substantially less favourable' when a pregnant employee is moved to alternative employment rather than being suspended required the employer to continue flight allowances to aircraft cabin crew when they were grounded because of pregnancy.

? Question

Following an evening out at the Flying Horse, Alice Heywood went home with Bill Johnson, a very personable young man with whom she spent the night. Bill and Alice did not see much of each other after the night of unbridled passion; however, the liaison produced a very healthy son.

Bill worked as a groundsman for a Premier League football club and, despite having little or nothing to do with Alice and his son, requested two weeks' parental leave to go on a golfing holiday with his pals. The leave was requested during a period of heavy fixtures, and the football club refused the request. The football club offered as a compromise a period during the summer months.

What are Bill's rights?

Solution !

Bill is the father of a son with whom he does not live. He requested two weeks' parental leave to go on a golfing holiday, which was refused because of the demands of the employer. An alternative date, however, was offered.

The Maternity and Parental Leave Regulations 1999 give an employee with a year's continuous service the right to take 13 weeks' unpaid parental leave. The conditions for eligibility are that the employee must have, or expects to have, 'parental responsibility' for the child and must take the leave in the first five years of the child's life. Parental responsibility will arise where the parent's name appears on the birth certificate (that is, residence with the child is irrelevant).

Bill wishes to exercise his entitlement to parental leave, not to spend time with his son, but moreover to go on holiday (that is, he wishes simply to take unpaid leave). Although the Act is silent on the purposes for which parental leave is available, it will not be interpreted within the spirit of the Act to allow Bill to take time off for a reason completely unconnected with the child. It is likely, therefore, that the club could have refused his request altogether.

Notwithstanding his motives, the club, although refusing the initial request, offered an alternative date. The Regulations provide that at least 21 days' notice must be given to the employer for the request, but that the employer may postpone the leave where taking it would cause disruption to the business.

If the request for leave is postponed, an alternative date must be given within six months, and the employer must notify the employee of this within seven days.

In the circumstances, it would appear that Bill has very little scope to complain. The club probably could have refused the request altogether, but has instead exercised its right to postpone.

Question

Edna works for Crash Ltd, a local driving school, as a driving instructor. Edna has been with Crash Ltd for seven months and has three children under the age of six. Edna has childcare commitments and so made a flexible working request to Crash Ltd to reduce the number of hours she worked by 50 per cent.

Crash Ltd has a policy that instructors are not able to reduce the hours they work below full-time until they have completed a year's service. Crash Ltd requires instructors to complete a certain number of hours' driving before they reach an acceptable standard. Edna's request was rejected on those grounds.

Edna has now made a complaint that Crash Ltd has discriminated against her by refusing the flexible working request.

Has Crash Ltd discriminated against Edna?

Solution

By having a policy that all instructors work full-time for the first year of their employment, Crash Ltd has applied a requirement that applies equally to all instructors whether male or female. This is known as a 'provision, criterion or practice' (PCP) within the Sex Discrimination Act 1975:

> s1(2)(b) a person discriminates against a woman if—
> (b)   he applies to her a provision, criterion or practice which he applies or would apply equally to a man, but—
>   (i)   which puts or would put women at a particular disadvantage when compared with men,
>   (ii)   which puts her at that disadvantage, and
>   (iii) which he cannot show to be a proportionate means of achieving a legitimate aim.

Edna's argument is that the PCP puts her at a disadvantage as compared to her male colleagues owing to her childcare commitments, which make her less able to comply with the full-time requirement.

It is generally accepted that more women than men have childcare commitments and as such are less able to comply with a requirement to work full-time. Crash Ltd must therefore show that the PCP is justified; that is, it is a 'proportionate means of achieving a legitimate aim'.

Crash Ltd has advised Edna that the reason for the full-time requirement is on health and safety grounds and that instructors should achieve a certain number of hours' driving within their first year's employment.

Is health and safety a strong enough justification for rejecting the request? In the case of *Starmer* v. *British Airways* (2005) a female pilot requested a 50 per cent reduction in the number of hours she worked. BA rejected this on the grounds of safety (that all pilots must achieve 2,000 flying hours before they are able to reduce the numbers of hours worked from full-time) and difficulty in reallocating resources. The Employment Appeal Tribunal (EAT) found that BA had not been justified in applying the PCP and that the employee had been discriminated against. The EAT found that the reasons for rejecting the request did not outweigh the seriousness of the disproportionate impact of the PCP, and therefore did not justify it.

How will Crash Ltd be able to show safety is a strong enough reason? Crash Ltd will need to adduce evidence to show that there is a real safety risk if instructors do not achieve a certain number of hours' driving within their first year of employment and that this would lead to a negative effect on their performance. This is likely to be difficult.

How could Crash Ltd have avoided this situation? Crash Ltd should not have applied the requirement to work full-time hours (the PCP) for the first year's employment unless it was able to show that this requirement was reasonably necessary. If it was able to show that it was reasonably necessary, the PCP may have been justified as long as it was a proportionate means of achieving a legitimate aim: protecting the safety of the instructors and their pupils.

Flexible working applications should also be considered on an individual basis. It is likely that each request will be different from the next and so should be considered on its merits.

There are eight specific business grounds on which a flexible working application can be rejected and these should always be considered and form the basis for any refusal. These grounds are:

- burden of additional costs;
- detrimental effect on ability to meet customer demand;
- inability to reorganize work among existing staff;
- inability to recruit additional staff;
- detrimental impact on quality;
- detrimental impact on performance;

- insufficiency of work during the periods the employee proposes to work;
- planned structural changes.

Crash Ltd has stated as its reason for refusal that it 'requires instructors to complete a certain number of hours' driving before they reach an acceptable standard'. This may enable Crash Ltd to claim that it rejected Edna's request based on the permissible ground of detrimental impact on quality and/or detrimental impact on performance.

In conclusion, Crash Ltd may be able to show that it refused flexible working on a permissible ground but that it was not justified in discriminating against Edna. It is therefore essential to fully explore the justification for a refusal of flexible working, even if it seems to comply with a permissible business ground.

? Question

Anisa is a shift worker who works a three-week shift pattern that is amended every month or two to meet seasonal demand. Anisa has two children under five years old and has asked you to calculate precisely how many working days she can have off for her maximum annual eight weeks' unpaid parental leave this year.

How would you approach this?

Solution !

Anisa is right that she is entitled to four weeks' unpaid leave per child under five years old per year (up to a maximum of 13 weeks per child in total). Under statutory rules you are not obliged to allow single days of unpaid parental leave to be taken. Leave must be taken in at least one-week blocks under the statutory scheme (The Maternity and Parental Leave Regulations, 1999).

The entitlement is based on the employee's normal working week or, if there are irregular shift or seasonal patterns, a 'normal' week is calculated by dividing the total working days per year (not deducting contractual or statutory holidays) by 52 (weeks).

In Anisa's case it may not be possible to calculate the total working days per year. You would therefore need to work out what a normal week would be in the particular season based on the best information you have and the appropriate shift patterns. If Anisa is most likely to have worked 19 days over a four-week period in that season, she would be entitled to time off equivalent to 4.75 days per week (19 divided by 4).

A week off is worked out from the 'normal' figure and would be based on the shift pattern for that particular week. You are not required to include abnormal overtime in your calculations, as the entitlement is to a normal working week. It would be as well to seek to agree the calculation with Anisa and to confirm the agreement in writing to avoid future complications.

It is worth while putting in place a workplace parental leave scheme that is no less favourable than the statutory minimum to ensure that there are no ambiguities and that all employees are treated fairly.

Question

Mary, a secretary at Courts R Us Solicitors, is due to return from maternity leave next week. Marianne, the human resources manager, receives a letter from Mary stating that she will not be able to return to work as planned since she is still breastfeeding and needs to be at home to feed her son. Marianne replies to the letter, informing Mary that unless she returns to work as planned, her absence will be considered unauthorized and will be dealt with under their disciplinary procedure. On receiving this letter, Mary telephones Marianne and explains that in the circumstances she has no alternative but to resign.

What potential claim(s) may Mary have against Courts R Us Solicitors?

Solution

Mary could make a claim for constructive unfair dismissal. To do this, she needs to show that the company acted in breach of contract: here, she is likely to argue that by refusing her request without discussion, the company is in breach of the duty of mutual trust and confidence.

There is a risk that if she resigns she may claim that she was forced to do so, owing to the company's actions, and bring a claim for constructive unfair dismissal. She may also claim direct sex discrimination, arguing that the company would have treated a man making a similar request (for example, to care for a sick relative) more favourably. She would, however, need to have some evidence for this, such as how a male employee had been treated in the past.

She may also bring a claim for indirect sex discrimination on the basis that she was unable to work her contractual hours owing to the need to breastfeed her baby and argue that the company applied a 'provision, criterion, or practice' which has a disproportionate impact on women because they are more likely than men to have primary childcare responsibilities. Unless the company can objectively justify the requirement, she is likely to succeed in her sex discrimination claim.

In order to defend any potential claim we need to be able to show that the company did everything to resolve the situation with Mary and considered any alternative arrangements, for example flexible working, taking a period of parental leave etc.

Therefore, on receiving Mary's letter the company should have suggested having a meeting either at the office, her home or a neutral location to discuss the issue. If she has a problem with childcare, then Marianne should have suggested that she bring her baby to the meeting.

In order to resolve the situation, Marianne could have suggested that Mary uses her annual leave entitlement or treats the time off as parental leave. This is unpaid leave and can last for up to four weeks.

Another alternative is for Mary to make an application for flexible working, where she can require the company to consider changing her working hours. The company must comply with the statutory procedure and give reasons for any refusal. Although the company is entitled to refuse a flexible working request, provided it is for one of the prescribed reasons, it should be careful not to adopt a potentially discriminatory policy by insisting her job cannot be performed on a part-time basis.

Note also that in order to make any claim, Mary would first need to raise a grievance in writing with the company, and wait 28 days before making a claim to a Tribunal. This could be done by a resignation letter. The company would then need to follow the procedure, by inviting Mary to a meeting.

? Question

Since giving birth, Melanie, a sales rep, has had post-natal depression. She was due to return to work from her maternity leave on 1 June but has been signed off work sick for the last six months. John, the managing director, says enough is enough and tells you that he wants to dismiss Melanie.

Can he do this?

Solution !

Employees who are dismissed for a pregnancy-related illness at any time prior to the end of the statutory maternity leave period will be able to claim that the dismissal is automatically unfair under the

Maternity and Parental Leave Regulations 1991. This will also amount to direct sex discrimination.

However, the Regulations make it clear that an employee is not protected from a childbirth-related dismissal that occurs after the end of the maternity leave period. Therefore, since Melanie's maternity leave period ended on 1 June, dismissing her for an illness arising out of pregnancy or childbirth, namely post-natal depression, will not be automatically unfair. Obviously, the ordinary unfair dismissal principles apply to determine the fairness of the dismissal as well as the statutory disciplinary and dismissal procedures. Therefore, John should ensure that he consults with Melanie, obtains medical evidence and considers any alternative positions within the company for Melanie. In the light of the medical evidence, John should also consider whether Melanie's condition might amount to a disability under the Disability Discrimination Act (DDA) (1995).

When calculating Melanie's absence, the company should not take any absence from the beginning of her pregnancy to the end of her maternity leave into account, as otherwise the dismissal may amount to sex discrimination.

In respect of a potential sex discrimination claim, Melanie's dismissal will be compared to that of a sick man in the company. In order to defend any claim the company has to be able to show that it would have dismissed a man in the same or similar circumstances as Melanie.

Question

Jane has worked as a cashier at Bargain Basement Superstore for nine months. Last month she informed the human resources manager that she was pregnant. Last week Jane was seen putting stock from the shop into her handbag at work and after a disciplinary investigation and hearing she was dismissed for gross misconduct. In the letter terminating her employment, the human resources manager informs her that because she has been dismissed for gross misconduct she is not entitled to receive Statutory Maternity Pay (SMP).

Is she correct?

Solution

Provided Jane has satisfied the conditions for payment of SMP as set out below, she will be entitled to receive SMP for the full 26-week period regardless of her misconduct. In order to be eligible for SMP Jane must have:

- worked for the employer for a continuous period of 26 weeks ending with the qualifying week, ie the 15th week before the expected week of childbirth (EWC);
- become pregnant and have reached the start of the 11th week before EWC;
- given 28 days' notice to her employer of the date when she expects liability to pay SMP will begin or, if not reasonably practicable, such lesser notice as was reasonably practicable;
- produced medical evidence of her pregnancy and expected date of EWC.

Question

You have an employee, Maria, who previously worked in your London office but has gone to your Cuban office for a season. She has now advised you that she is pregnant and wishes to return to the UK before she is no longer able to fly back (the Civil Aviation rules state that pregnant women cannot fly once they are 28 weeks pregnant) because she does not want to have the baby in Cuba. Maria has three weeks' holiday accrued but unused. Maria wants to continue working and has asked that you find her a role in the London office as soon as possible so that she may return and work over here.

You do not have a role for Maria in the UK; can you make her start her maternity leave early?

Solution

Maria has decided that she does not want to continue working in Cuba but there is no job for her in the UK and she does not want to start her maternity leave until two weeks before the baby is due to be born.

Do you have to find Maria a job in the UK?

Whilst you may sympathize with Maria's situation, Maria is employed to perform a role, which is based in Cuba. If Maria is now unwilling to continue in that role you are under no duty to provide her with an alternative role, even if the reason for her request is her pregnancy.

Can Maria say she is returning on health and safety grounds? Does this matter?

Maria may try to argue that she will be unable to fly once she is 28 weeks pregnant; however, this is not an issue for the company. If Maria wants to have her baby in the UK she will simply have to fly back before then. There is no health and safety requirement that will require the company to bring Maria home to have the child in the UK rather than in Cuba.

Can you offer Maria any kind of assistance?

Maria hasn't taken any holiday yet so she could fly home at 28 weeks, take the holiday she has accrued prior to her maternity leave (approximately 3 weeks) and then start her maternity leave at the earliest date (11 weeks prior to the expected week of childbirth).

This is the only solution that the company will be able to offer Maria if she insists on returning to the UK because there are no other roles available for her. However, the company cannot force Maria to do this. An employee can only be 'forced' into beginning her maternity leave if she is absent on sick leave for pregnancy-related reasons in the four weeks prior to the expected week of childbirth. If this occurs, the maternity leave will automatically begin then.

You should also consider whether Maria might have any grounds for bringing a sex discrimination case against you. Could she argue that you have treated male employees seconded abroad, who wanted to return to the UK early, more favourably than you are treating her?

See also page 42.

Chapter 9

Working time

? Question

You are the HR manager of Scrooge's Season's Greetings Limited, a company that produces and distributes greetings cards. Your company's holiday year runs from 1 January to 31 December. At the beginning of October, the managers realize that the production site is understaffed and that the company is going to struggle to get all the cards out in time for Christmas. They ask you to issue a notice to all employees telling them that they can't book any holidays between now and Christmas. Your contract does not allow employees to carry unused holiday into the following year; the managers do not want to make an exception to this rule this year and neither do they want to pay employees for their lost holidays.

Can you get away with it?

Solution !

Can you prevent your employees from taking holiday between now and the end of the year?

The Working Time Regulations (1998) allow employers to instruct their employees that they may not take holiday during certain parts of the year, provided they give them notice of the same length as the period they want them not to take holiday for (Regulation 15(4)(b)). Put another way, if you want to prevent your employees from taking holiday over a period of 13 weeks, you would have to give them 13 weeks' notice under the Working Time Regulations. Therefore, clearly you do not have time to give employees that notice in this case.

However, the Regulations also allow employers to turn down individual requests for holiday, provided they do so within the correct time limit.

Under the Regulations, workers have to give you notice of their requests to take holiday of double the length of time they are requesting off (Regulation 15(4)(a)). Or, to put it more simply, if a worker wants two weeks' holiday, he or she has to give his or her employer four weeks' notice. The employer then has the chance (under Regulation 15(4)(b)) to issue the worker with a counter notice denying his or her request and that has to be given with notice of the same length as the period of the holiday requested.

So, if the employee wants two weeks' holiday, he or she has to give the employer four weeks' notice. If the employer wants to refuse that holiday, it has to give the employee two weeks' notice of that refusal.

Therefore, although you will not be able to give a blanket prohibition on employees taking holiday between now and Christmas under the Working Time Regulations, you can turn down holiday requests as they come in, provided you do so in time. Of course, the fact that you cannot give a blanket prohibition under the Regulations does not prevent you from announcing to your employees that you intend to refuse holiday requests over that period. Your own contracts of employment may also back this up if they make it clear that the company reserves the right to refuse requests for leave if they conflict with the needs of the business.

If you do prevent your employees from taking their holiday, will you have to pay them their accrued, but untaken, holiday entitlements at the end of the holiday year or allow them to roll the holiday over into the next holiday year? The Working Time Regulations are silent on this point. If a worker's contract terminates during a holiday year, they are entitled to be paid for their accrued, but untaken, holiday entitlements. However, the Working Time Regulations do not require employers to pay their employees for any accrued but untaken holiday pay at the end of the holiday year.

The European Court of Justice ruled in 2006 that although nothing in the Working Time Directive prohibited the carrying over of part or all the minimum annual leave entitlement, payment in lieu is prohibited by art 7(2), which states that minimum annual leave cannot be replaced by cash unless the employment relationship ends (*Federatie Nederlandse Vakbeweging* v. *Nederlands*).

Therefore, legally, the managers can get away with it! In reality, telling employees that they will not be allowed to take any holiday between October and the end of the year, and that they will get nothing in return, may cause some unrest and you may want to try to persuade the managers to consider offering some sort of sugaring of the pill. However, they are not legally obliged to do so.

? Question

An employee who has just had his holiday request turned down has suggested you should change your holiday policy to give priority to employees with children to allow them to take holiday at the same time as their children.

Is this a good idea?

Solution !

Provided you do not discriminate against any protected group, and provided you comply with the Working Time Regulations, you can operate whatever policy you like for accepting or rejecting holiday requests. Most organizations operate a 'first come, first served' system. Others allow employees who have had their holiday requests turned down in one year to get first refusal on popular holiday dates the year after.

The system suggested by this employee is for employees with children to get first refusal over popular holiday dates every year. If you instigate this system, it may be unpopular with employees who do not have any children, but will those employees actually have any grounds for a claim?

It is well established that the law of sex discrimination provides a basis for female employees to seek family-friendly policies from their employers, on the basis that women are more likely than men to have primary responsibility for childcare and so an employer's failure to accommodate the childcare needs of employees will disadvantage a greater proportion of women than men. However, the person asking the question here is male so this will not apply.

The Sex Discrimination Act 1975 also prohibits discrimination against married people (but not single people), and it may be possible for a male employee in these circumstances to claim that this is indirect discrimination against married people, as they are more likely to have children than single people. The key question is then whether the employer can justify the policy of treating all holiday requests in the same way.

In December 2003, the concept of sexual orientation discrimination was introduced into UK employment law by the Employment Equality (Sexual Orientation) Regulations 2003. Under the Regulations, a worker can claim indirect sexual orientation discrimination if his employer applies a practice that puts employees at a particular disadvantage on grounds of their sexuality. So if the employer refused to introduce such a policy, it could be argued that this was indirect discrimination against heterosexual people, assuming it could be shown that heterosexual people were more likely to have children than homosexual people. Conversely, if the employer did introduce such a policy, it might be indirect discrimination against homosexual people, if they could show they were less likely to have children than heterosexual people! The key question would be whether the employer could justify the policy. In this case, if a homosexual employee did challenge the practice, the employer would have to show that it was a proportionate means for achieving a legitimate aim.

Here, the legitimate aim would be allowing employees who have children to have time off work at the same time as their children's school holidays. Doing so might make sound business sense if (which is likely) it could be shown that employees with children would be more content and more likely to stay if they were able regularly to take holidays at the same times as their children.

The means of achieving that aim are probably proportionate. If the needs of the organization are such that employees' holiday requests cannot always be accommodated, and it is not possible to ensure that employees with children are able to take holidays at the same time as their children in any other way, the suggestion of allowing employees with young children first refusal on popular holiday dates every year would probably be justified and so would not be unlawful sexual orientation discrimination.

Question

You employ Dave to drive around the South East visiting clients. During the day, you call Dave on his mobile phone to add new appointments to his round.

Dave's working day finishes when he has finished all of his appointments. For a while, Dave took to turning his mobile phone off during the day to avoid new appointments. You told Dave he must have his mobile phone on at all times unless he is actually doing a delivery or driving around town.

Dave has threatened to sue under the Working Time Regulations. He thinks his working weeks, which include frequent overnight stays in hotels, average around 70 hours a week and his job is ruining his family life. You have told Dave you believe his working hours are actually quite short, as he spends only about two hours of every day in appointments and the rest of the time he is just driving. Anyway, you say, he can't sue under the Working Time Regulations.

Who is right? What issues may arise?

Solution

If Dave is working more than 48 hours per week averaged over 17 weeks, you may be in breach of the Working Time Regulations.

Working time is 'any period during which the worker is working, at his employer's disposal and carrying out his activities or duties'. All the time Dave spends driving between appointments is working time. The time Dave spends on overnight stays, however, should not count towards his working time. Although he is away from his home and family during that time, he is not on call and he is still free to do his own thing.

It is true to say that Dave cannot sue under the Working Time Regulations – the Regulations are policed by the Health & Safety Executive and fines for breaching the 48-hour working week can only be imposed by them. However, he could bring an action for breach of contract (although this can only lead to an injunction, not to any compensation – *Barber & ors* v. *RJB Mining (UK) Limited* (1999)).

In the case of *Owen* v. *Smith Walker & ors* (1999), a worker who was working in excess of the 48-hour limit and whose employer did not have a system in place to monitor his hours was allowed to resign and claim unfair constructive dismissal.

In addition, the mobile phone may be a problem. Legislation was introduced in December 2003 making it an offence to use mobile phones while driving. Employers who encourage or force their employees to use mobile phones will also be liable. Even if the car is stationary, for example at traffic lights or in traffic jams, drivers must not use mobile phones and you must not encourage them to do so.

If you want your employees to answer their mobile phones while driving, you will have to provide them with legally compliant hands-free kits. These are kits which are fixed to a cradle and fitted to the car's audio system. Phones with earpieces and microphones are not legally compliant.

Chapter 10

Dismissal

Question

Shane is a storeman. His job involves some heavy lifting. His absence record is worse than average, but not the worst you have. Most of his absences have been of three or four days and uncertificated. He has, in relation to those, given a variety of reasons – cold, headache, stomach bug. Twice, over the last three years, his reason has been 'a bad back'.

Three weeks ago he went off with 'a bad back' and has submitted medical certificates on which the only word of the diagnosis you can actually make out is 'lumbar'. The first certificate was for one week. Then there was one for four weeks: that still has two weeks to run. One of your supervisors has just reported seeing Shane in the local DIY superstore with a trolley loaded up with wallpaper and paint.

What, if anything, should you do?

Solution

The reported sighting of Shane in the circumstances described proves nothing, but it does raise a sufficient question for you to be reasonably entitled to investigate further.

Prima facie, being 'with' a trolley might suggest that Shane was pushing it and, perhaps, had loaded it. But that is only one possible interpretation. You need more detail from the supervisor if he or she can provide it. What, if any, physical activity was Shane involved in during the sighting? Was he seen lifting things onto the trolley? If so, what sort of things, in terms of bulk and weight and awkwardness? Was Shane seen pushing the trolley? If not, was anybody else with him who might have been doing any lifting and/or pushing? How did Shane appear in terms of his mobility and agility? Did Shane see the supervisor? Did the supervisor speak to Shane? If so, what was said? If you think, in the light of any such details, that there are grounds for taking the investigation further, the details should be recorded in writing. This might be done by the supervisor giving a detailed written statement: at the very least you should make notes of what you have been told and get those agreed – after amendment if necessary – by the supervisor's signature.

That his doctor has advised him not to work does not necessarily mean that Shane has to stay at home. If, however, it seems that Shane is acting inconsistently with his reported state of health, this raises questions as to whether his state of health is better than it is reported to be – even, perhaps, so good that he would be capable of working, and/or whether his activities are likely to delay his recovery.

These are, essentially, medical questions. But the answers to medical questions depend upon the evidence on which they are based and patients do not always give their doctors all that evidence. The answers may also differ depending on the perspective, and knowledge, of the doctor. Shane's own doctor's prime duty is to his or her patient and, where there is any doubt, Shane is likely to be given the benefit of it: also, the doctor must rely on what Shane says for information about precisely what his job involves, hence whether his condition precludes him from doing it. If your company has a medical adviser, he or she may take a more sceptical view of any reported symptoms which are not backed up by what a physical examination can reveal; also, he or she may know, or can be briefed, about the detailed physical requirements of Shane's job.

If what you learn from the supervisor leaves you with any reasonable doubt that Shane is acting consistently with his reported state of health, you need to consider whether, before seeking any medical opinion, there is further evidence you can gather. In extreme cases employers (or, for example, insurers paying out benefits on their behalf) have engaged private detectives to report on and collect video evidence of employees' mobility. Provided that no illegal methods are used, this does not involve any breach of the claimant's human rights. In a case where abuse of the sick pay scheme is suspected, it may be a proportionate response to hire a private investigator. In addition, particularly if you have a practice of making 'welfare' visits to sick employees' homes, you may consider making such a call, unannounced, on Shane.

Unless (which is unlikely) your investigations produce unequivocal evidence that Shane has no back problem (or other debilitating condition) at all, you will need to get professional medical advice, in the light of your evidence, on the two questions above. You might do this from:

- your company medical adviser, if you have one;
- Shane's own doctor; or
- both.

If you have a company medical adviser, you should go there first. Depending on the relationship, you may be able to have an informal chat about whether the evidence you have collected could raise any doubts in medical terms and, if it does, about the best way of resolving these. If your medical adviser says that he or she cannot give any opinion without examining Shane and/or getting a report from Shane's doctor, you will need to get consents from Shane.

Whether you wish to, and can, initiate any action against Shane and, if so, what, will depend on your assessment of the evidence in the light of any medical advice you receive. Experience suggests that such medical advice – even from the employer's own medical adviser – seldom provides the sort of unequivocal answer that the employer would like. But any decision that has to be made is a management decision, not a medical one, although it should take account of the medical evidence.

If you believe that Shane has been guilty of any misconduct – or even just of inappropriate behaviour, in not taking all reasonable steps to speed his recovery – you will need to bring this to his attention. If you feel that your evidence is strong enough to sustain a disciplinary charge – for example, that Shane is guilty of abusing your sick pay scheme by claiming ill-health when he was not genuinely ill – you will need to arrange for a formal disciplinary hearing to be held. Again, dependant on the strength of evidence, dismissal or a lesser sanction may be the outcome of the disciplinary hearing.

See also page 47.

UNFAIR DISMISSAL

Question

Altaf has been a senior employee within a local authority for many years. He has always performed his work to a satisfactory standard and has never been the subject of disciplinary proceedings, or similar proceedings relating to his standard of work.

However, throughout his time with the organization, Altaf has had an attitude problem. He has declined to help other employees when they have asked, is condescending towards less experienced employees, is disrespectful towards his superiors, and reacts negatively and excessively when any question or comment whatsoever about his work is raised. Various people at the organization are fed up with Altaf and want to know if you can dismiss employees because of an attitude problem.

Can you do this?

Solution !

There are six fair reasons for dismissal, of which three may be relevant here: capability, conduct and some other substantial reason.

It is likely that some aspects of Altaf's behaviour are serious enough to be categorized as misconduct, although many of the complaints about him, such as a reluctance to assist with colleagues, may not sit comfortably within the accepted definition of misconduct. It is difficult for an employer to point to a specific rule that the employee had broken by reason of his unhelpful attitude towards his fellow employees. Generally speaking, misconduct does equate with the breaking of an identifiable rule.

Some elements of Altaf's behaviour may come within the definition of capability, in that, arguably, to be a fully functioning employee, and discharging his duties to his best ability, he needs to have a reasonable working relationship with colleagues. Again, however, it is stretching the point somewhat to make the attitude problem fit within the generally accepted definition of capability.

This leads to the third element, some other substantial reason. In a reasonably extreme case, where there is a severe attitude problem leading to a breakdown in working relationships, it may be some other substantial reason to dismiss.

In the case of *Perkin* v. *St. George's Healthcare NHS Trust* (2005), the Court of Appeal decided that an employee's personality itself cannot be a potentially fair reason. But, where the personality causes serious problems in the relationship between a senior employee (in Mr Perkin's case, Director of Finance of a large NHS Trust) and 'stakeholders', including senior management, colleagues and third parties, this can lead to an irretrievable breakdown in the working relationship. Altaf's behaviour could therefore amount to 'some other substantial reason' and grounds for a fair dismissal.

Even if the dismissal procedure followed is unfair (as in *Perkin* v. *St George's*), it is possible that any compensation for unfair dismissal can be significantly reduced, even to zero, for 'blameworthy' conduct on the part of an employee.

In Mr Perkin's case, his conduct during the disciplinary process included ill-founded attacks on colleagues' honesty, financial probity and integrity that made it quite impossible for him to work with them again. The Court of Appeal accepted that the Employment Tribunal was able to rely on the case of *Polkey* v. *AE Dayton Services Ltd* (1988) in finding that Mr Perkin would have been 100 per cent likely to be dismissed had a fair procedure been followed. The Employment Tribunal therefore correctly awarded him no compensation at all, for 'contributory fault', despite it finding that Mr Perkin was unfairly dismissed.

As far as Altaf is concerned, if his conduct prior to a disciplinary procedure has led to a serious breakdown in working relationships, it is possible that you could fairly dismiss him for some other substantial reason. Since Altaf reacts negatively and excessively when challenged, it also seems quite likely that his attitude problem would continue into disciplinary proceedings. Any disciplinary proceeding may, of itself, result in a serious breakdown in working relationships and a fair dismissal at the end – or possibly an unfair dismissal with a reduced chance of significant (or any) compensation.

Question

You overhear a loud argument between an employee and her manager, at the end of which the employee screams 'I'm not working here anymore, I resign!' and storms out.

The next day the employee comes to you and says she did not mean to resign. What do you do?

Solution

If an employee utters words of resignation in circumstances where the employer knows, or ought to have known, that the employee might not have meant them, then the employer is obliged to give the employee a reasonable opportunity to clarify the 'resignation'. If the employee makes it clear within that reasonable period that she did not intend to resign, then the employer must have the employee back. If the employer refuses to have her back, that refusal amounts to a dismissal, which will probably be an unfair dismissal – *Sovereign House Security Services Ltd* v. *Savage* (1989). However, if the employee returns to work, you may wish to take disciplinary procedures against her, on the grounds of misconduct.

Question

You are walking through the park at lunchtime and you spot one of your employees, Tim, playing with his children. Tim has phoned in sick with a 'tummy bug'. He has a bad sickness record and is being paid company sick pay. He has nearly exhausted his 10 days' annual entitlement.

What do you do?

Solution

There are two linked issues here, unauthorized absence and abuse of the contractual sick pay terms. This is not an 'absence from work due to sickness' case, although at first glance it looks like one, and it is easy to be sidetracked by these issues. We are not dealing with Tim's health. Rather, we are dealing with his attendance.

Unauthorized absence

If an employee is 'off sick' but in fact is well, this is unauthorized absence, which is misconduct. In the normal way there should be an investigation. You are the witness, so should write out a statement, which you will give to the person conducting the investigation. You cannot hear the disciplinary hearing which follows as you are a witness to the alleged misconduct.

As in all misconduct cases, an employer can make a decision based on genuine and honest belief after reasonable investigation (*British Home Stores* v. *Burchell* (1980)). If an employer reasonably concludes that an employee was lying, it can act accordingly; there does not have to be absolute proof of lying. If the employer feels that the absence was unjustified, a warning may result if this was the first time. If the employee claims that he was ill when he rang in but 'got better' later in the day, or otherwise comes up with an unsatisfactory response, the employer will have to make a judgement as to how seriously it regards this misconduct. His attendance history is of limited relevance, as we are dealing with a misconduct allegation rather than attendance as such. We feel that to dismiss Tim in this instance would result in an unfair dismissal unless there are aggravating factors that we do not know about. The misconduct, as described in the question, is probably not serious enough to justify dismissal if it is a one-off.

Sick pay terms

Tim has been paid sick pay but if he was not in fact sick this could be considered fraudulent, and as such needs to be included in the disciplinary hearing as described above. Contractual sick pay policies should always either be discretionary or have terms enabling the employer not to pay if there is a lack of evidence of genuine sickness, or if the conditions of the absence policy are not met. In the event your sickness policy does not state this, it would be an idea to amend your sickness policy to ensure that it does. Here, the employer may (if the sick pay policy allows) refuse to pay sick pay, so that the day in question becomes in effect unpaid leave in addition to any disciplinary action.

Question

Mike, who works as a salesman, has complained that his job is 'stressing him out'. He has started taking lots of time off work and his doctor's certificates all give 'stress' as the reason. Mike has asked for an assistant to help him to cope. Mike's manager, who is not known for his sympathetic nature, has said: 'If Mike can't take the stress, I don't want him. Tell him he should clear off and go and work in a library!'

What should you do? What are the risks if you do nothing?

Solution

Stress can lead to unsatisfactory performance by an employee. However, if you are contemplating dismissing Mike, the question of whether that dismissal was fair or not would be determined by the application of the normal principles.

If you dismiss Mike without properly consulting him, or giving proper consideration to what steps you could take to alleviate the stress but allow him to carry on working, that dismissal would probably be deemed unfair.

You should talk to Mike about what he wants. You should consider whether you can accommodate Mike's requests – in particular, you might consider whether it would be possible to take on an assistant to help him cope or whether there are any other roles Mike could do that would be less stressful. Of course, there are limits to what you will be prepared to do but you could make that clear to Mike from the outset.

Stress itself is not an illness. However, certain stress-related conditions can qualify as disabilities. Therefore, dismissing Mike could lead to a disability discrimination claim as well as an unfair dismissal claim. You should seek a report from Mike's doctor (subject to permission from Mike under the Access to Medical Reports Act 1988) and consider whether there are any reasonable adjustments that you could make in order to allow Mike to carry on working. One reasonable adjustment might be providing Mike with the assistant he wants. However (as above), this might be too expensive and therefore not reasonable. Another reasonable adjustment might be providing Mike with some degree of counselling or some additional support at times of particularly high stress.

Therefore, it would be a mistake simply to dismiss Mike quickly as his manager has suggested.

However, there are some risks to doing nothing. Employers have a duty to take reasonable care of the health and safety of their employees, and that includes their mental health. If Mike goes on to suffer psychological injury as a result of this stress, he may bring a personal injury claim against the organization.

In the case of *Walker* v. *Northumberland County Council* (1995), the High Court ordered a county council to pay damages to an ex-employee on the basis that, as employers, they had a duty not to cause him psychiatric damage by giving him too much work and insufficient backup support. Damages of £175,000 were reportedly agreed in that case.

Stress itself is not an illness and, in order to win such a claim, Mike would have to show that his stress caused a recognized disorder or psychiatric illness. In the 2002 House of Lords case of *Hatton* v. *Sutherland* it was confirmed that a worker could win a stress related injury claim only if the stress was obvious to the employer, the harm was reasonably foreseeable and the employer really ought to have done something about it. That case also established that no job is intrinsically stressful and employers are entitled to assume that their employees can withstand the normal stresses involved in their jobs.

Therefore, although you are probably safe if Mike tries to bring a stress-related injury claim now, you are effectively on warning that Mike has a problem with stress and, if you do nothing, a stress-related injury claim may arise and could succeed in the future. You should take Mike's complaint seriously, talk to him about why he feels his job is so stressful, what aspects of his job he finds stressful and what he feels could be done to alleviate the stress he is feeling. You should also try to get a medical report on Mike's condition.

Ultimately, if it turns out that Mike simply does not have the mettle to cope with the job, you would be better to dismiss Mike on the grounds of capability or demote him into another job with less responsibility than do nothing. However, there are dangers in trying to do so too quickly.

See also page 189.

❓ Question

You have been asked by one of the company's managers to make one of his team 'redundant' because he is not performing. He has suggested a lump sum payment and a compromise agreement. He wants to know if he can tell the employee what is planned.

What advice would you give?

Solution !

It must be explained that underperformance is not a ground for redundancy and the potentially fair reason for dismissal would need to be capability. However, it is now difficult in these circumstances simply to present the employee with a compromise agreement (CA) and rely on the 'without prejudice' (WP) rule. If this method is used, the employee can argue that the WP rule doesn't apply because there is no existing dispute between the parties. WP operates only where there is a genuine attempt to settle a dispute. No dispute – no rule.

This is not 'new law' as such but it is something that received some publicity a couple of years ago. In the 2004 case of *BNP Paribas* v. *Mezzotero* the employer called the employee to a meeting and, at the start of that meeting, invited her to agree to a 'without prejudice' discussion. This was before any question of the termination of her employment had been raised. The only prior context was her raising of a grievance about how her maternity leave, and her return from it, had been handled. For the first time, in that discussion, the suggestion was made that she should go – with a package of £100,000. The Employment Appeal Tribunal (EAT) upheld the Tribunal's decision that she was entitled – in support of a claim for sex discrimination and victimization – to adduce evidence of the suggestion at that meeting that her employment could be terminated.

The EAT agreed that the WP rule applies when there is an existing dispute between the parties and what is said/written involves a genuine attempt to compromise that dispute. The reason that it did not apply here was (principally) that the chairman was, on the evidence, entitled to conclude that there was no existing dispute concerning the continuation or otherwise of the employee's employment. Raising a grievance does not inevitably imply that an employee believes that his or her job is at risk.

In the circumstances of the question therefore, the presentation of a CA at this stage would give the employee potential grounds to resign and claim constructive dismissal. If he didn't resign and a capability review was entered into, the earlier offer of a compromise is likely to undermine the fairness of the whole process.

Thought needs to go into when a CA is offered. It is often relatively simple to make the employee request a WP conversation. Alternatively, if a cautious approach is required, the CA can be offered after the completion of an appropriate capability review. Debate still exists as to whether the mere initiation of such a procedure is a 'dispute'. Our view is that as long as the employer has made it clear that termination of employment under the procedure is a possible outcome, the employee believes that his or her job is at risk, and so the WP rule will apply.

It is also advisable for an employer to give itself an 'escape route' from a WP conversation that does not go well. In other words, if the offer is rejected, the employer then reverts to a formal process and effects a (hopefully) fair dismissal. If the offer was successfully made without prejudice, this means that the compromise agreement never comes to the attention of any subsequent Tribunal, which will therefore consider only the formal process. Clearly if the Tribunal sees the compromise agreement, the subsequent process will be exposed as a sham, rendering it almost certainly unfair.

See also page 190.

❓ Question

Aileen has been absent sick for eight months. She ran out of company sick pay three months ago. Shortly after that she moved back to live with her parents, 200 miles away. It has been obvious to everyone for some time that she was unlikely ever to return to work, but you wanted to get this properly medically confirmed before taking formal action. There have been delays in getting medical reports – some occasioned by your own medical adviser and some by Aileen's own doctors (including some hesitation by Aileen about giving the necessary consents). All reports have now been received and confirm that Aileen will not, in the foreseeable future, be fit to return to work in her old role or in any other that you have, or could make, available. You wrote to Aileen a week ago, telling her that you were contemplating her dismissal by reason of her incapability, enclosing the medical reports, and asking her to contact you to arrange a meeting to discuss the situation. You have just received her reply, which accuses you of unreasonable delay and also says: 'As I am currently on medication which makes it difficult for me to express myself, I must insist on my mother coming with me to the meeting to help me put my views across. In any event, as I now live in Devon, the only reasonable location for the meeting is Devon.'

What potential exposure have you here? In what, if any, respects have the statutory disciplinary procedures not been complied with?

Solution ❗

The statutory Disciplinary and Dismissal Procedure (DDP) requires that when an employer is contemplating dismissing an employee – including on capability grounds – it invites the employee to a meeting before making any decision. It also requires that:

- each step and action under the procedure must be taken without unreasonable delay;
- meetings must be conducted in such a way as to allow the employee to put his or her case; and
- timing and location of meetings must be reasonable.

Unreasonable delay

It is most unlikely that Aileen's complaint of unreasonable delay would be upheld by a Tribunal. This is because the DDP applies, under the Regulations, 'when an employer contemplates dismissing or taking relevant disciplinary action against an employee'. Although the employer has been gathering medical reports and so forth, in this context 'contemplates' must mean more than, simply, 'recognizes as possible': it must impute a 'proposal' to dismiss by the employer. Until an employer has not only recognized that dismissal is a possibility, but has also obtained the information on which – if it is to take place – it would be justifiable, it cannot be in a position to meet the requirements of Step One of the DDP. So time runs only from the point of 'contemplation of dismissal', not from the time the first report was obtained.

The same, somewhat technical, points – for example, about the meaning of 'contemplates' and, in effect, whether the 'unreasonable delay' referred to in the DPP can occur before Step One or only once Step One has been taken – will not be relevant in the broader context of unfair dismissal. It is, however, difficult to see how Aileen could persuade a Tribunal that a dismissal which would otherwise be fair could be rendered unfair simply because it occurred later rather than earlier. The cause of action is unfair *dismissal,* not unfair *retention in employment.*

Allowing Aileen to bring her mother

It has long been a basic principle of reasonableness for a worker to have the right to be accompanied by a companion in disciplinary hearings. It is now part of the Statutory Disciplinary and Dismissal Procedure and the right to be accompanied has been extended, under the ACAS Code of Practice, to cover any dismissal meeting.

Workers have the right to be accompanied by a colleague or a trade union official. Neither the Employment Relations Act 1999 nor the DDP entitles a worker to insist on any other representative coming with them to a meeting. Provided Aileen's contract of employment does not say anything different, she does not have the right to insist on her mother attending the meeting with her.

However, under the DDP, meetings must be 'conducted in a manner that enables both the employer and the employee to explain their cases'. If a Tribunal were to agree with Aileen's claim that she would not be able to express herself without her mother being present, then preventing her from bringing her mother could in itself be a breach of the DDP. Therefore, given the circumstances, the sensible course would probably be to allow Aileen's mother to accompany Aileen at the meeting.

Location and timing of meetings

The DDP's requirement that the location and timing of meetings must be reasonable will no doubt, over time, have some limits drawn for it by case law. In the meantime, it must be taken to imply that they cannot be held simply to suit one party's convenience. So, for instance, an employer would not be reasonable if it fixed meetings at times when the employee could not reasonably be expected to be available or at places which he or she could not reasonably be expected to find accessible. It is easy to envisage circumstances in which it would be reasonable for a meeting to take place at a neutral venue or at the employee's home; and unreasonable for an employer to refuse that. The employee, when working, travels on each working day from home to work so, if there was a good reason why the employee could not travel from home to work for a meeting, to ask the employer to travel from work to the employee's home for it does not, in principle, seem unreasonable.

It would probably not, however, in general be unreasonable for an employer to refuse to travel 200 miles so that a meeting could be held. It might be different if the employer had required Aileen to move from the address from which she attended work to her parents' address; or if the employer had premises, at which a manager competent to represent it in the proposed meeting was based or in regular attendance, within 'commuting distance' of Aileen's parents' home. But in the absence of such special factors, Aileen's suggestion is simply suiting *her* convenience. That is no more 'reasonable' than the employer simply suiting *its* convenience.

Within the context of the DDP, Aileen's inability to attend a meeting fixed for a reasonable time and location at or near her place of work is much more likely to mean that reg.11(3)(c) of the Employment Act 2002 (Dispute Resolution) Regulations 2004 will apply. Under that, where 'it is not practicable for the party to commence the procedure or comply with the subsequent requirement within a reasonable period', the procedure is regarded as having been completed with neither party being in default for the fact that, actually, it has not. This will not discharge the employer from the duty of acting 'reasonably' so far as the unfair dismissal law is concerned. It would therefore be sensible for Aileen, if she cannot attend a meeting, to be invited to write in with any information or arguments that she wishes to be considered before any dismissal decision is made. But for present purposes the point is that, whether that is done or not, the absence of a meeting will not render any dismissal automatically unfair by being in breach of the DDP.

❓ Question

You have employed a temp through an agency for 18 months; you now want to dispense with her services.

How do you go about it and what risks are there?

Solution ❗

Only employees have unfair dismissal rights. Workers do not. The risk here is that the agency worker with more than one year's service can argue that he or she is an employee rather than a worker, and therefore argue that he or she has the right not to be unfairly dismissed.

In *Dacas* v. *Brook Street Bureau (UK) Limited* (2004), the Court of Appeal held that a contract of employment may be implied between a hirer and an agency worker, despite the fact that there is an express clause stating that the agency worker is not an employee of either the hirer or the agency. The reason for this decision was because the hirer controlled what Mrs Dacas did, what time she came into work, and when she left. As a result of this high level of control over the agency worker, the Court of Appeal decided that there was an implied contract of employment between the hirer and Mrs Dacas, based on the reality of the relationship between all parties.

The approach in Dacas was strongly endorsed by the Court of Appeal in *Cable & Wireless Plc* v. *Muscat* (2006) and this approach seems likely to be followed in future cases on agency workers, though each case will depend upon its own circumstances: there must be mutuality, and control by the 'employer'.

Therefore, despite having an express clause to the contrary in the contract between the hirer, the agency worker and the agency, Tribunals may find that a contract of employment exists between the hirer and the agency worker. If agency workers are successful in arguing that they are employees rather than workers, and have more than 12 months' service, they can then go on to argue that they have a right not to be unfairly dismissed.

In the event that a dispute arises between the hirer and an agency worker with over 12 months' service, or if the hirer otherwise wants to end the contract, it is advisable to let the agency initiate the disciplinary or redundancy procedure from the outset. The hirer must ensure that the agency adopts a fair procedure. This will give you two lines of defence in the event the agency worker brings a subsequent claim for unfair dismissal:

1. First, by asking the agency to conduct the disciplinary or redundancy procedure and for you to take the 'back seat', you can argue in any subsequent claim that the agency worker was not your employee as you did not have a sufficient degree of control. By allowing the agency to conduct the disciplinary or redundancy procedure you are keeping the agency worker at 'arm's length'.
2. The second line of defence is that, if the Tribunal finds that the agency worker is in reality your employee (as in the Dacas case), by ensuring the agency adopts a fair and reasonable procedure you can simply argue that the employee was not unfairly dismissed as a fair and reasonable procedure had been followed.

Remember that any disciplinary or redundancy procedure carried out by the agency must be conducted in accordance with the statutory dismissal procedures to avoid any automatic unfair dismissal claims.

? Question

You are the HR manager of Hold Your Horses, a distributor of saddlery and riding gear. You have outlets in Norwich, Bedford, Reading, Guildford, Brighton and Dartford. As well as the shop front in each location, there are sales executives who travel around local horse shows and similar events promoting Hold Your Horses' products. These travelling sales executives have done well in all regions apart from Dartford, where there seem to be few functions to attend, so you decide to make Olivia, the Dartford sales executive, redundant. The sales executives at the other branches will be kept on. Olivia challenges her redundancy, saying that all of the sales executives at the different locations should have been put into one pool for redundancy, and compared with each other. She says that on that basis, given that she is the longest-serving sales executive, one of the others should have been made redundant ahead of her.

Is Olivia correct?

Would your answer be different if, instead of having branches many miles apart, all branches were clustered in one county, and were less than 10 miles apart?

Solution

1. Redundancy is exhaustively defined in Section 139(1) of the Employment Rights Act and the definition applies both to claims for redundancy payments and to unfair dismissal claims. The statutory words are:

   > For the purposes of this Act, an employee who is dismissed shall be taken to be dismissed by reason of redundancy if the dismissal is wholly or mainly attributable to:
   >
   > (a)   the fact that his employer has ceased or intends to cease – (i) to carry on the business for the purposes of which the employee was employed by him, or (ii) to carry on that business in the place where the employee was so employed; or
   >
   > (b)   the fact that the requirements of that business – (i) for employees to carry out work of a particular kind, or (ii) for employees to carry out work of a particular kind in the place where the employee was employed by the employer, have ceased or diminished or are expected to cease or diminish.

   In this case, Olivia's workplace has not closed, but there is a diminishing need for employees to do the work that she is employed to do, so her redundancy falls into that category. It is, therefore, under Section 139(1)(b).

2. In this case, of particular relevance to Olivia's situation are the words in the definition 'in the place where the employee was employed by the employer'. This brings it within sub-paragraph (ii) of that provision. The redundancy is taking place only in Dartford, and therefore only Olivia is affected by that redundancy decision. None of the other sales executives come into the equation at all. Olivia is, therefore, not correct in her claim that she should have been put into a pool with the others.

3. In order for this dismissal to be fair, you will need to consult with Olivia and consider alternative positions, but it seems to be a fairly straightforward redundancy situation.

4. The answer, however, might well be different if the shops were all close together. What does 'the place where the employee was

employed' mean in that situation? This can in some cases be a fairly complex analysis. Cases show that it can be widely defined to include a geographical area, influenced by both the employee's contract of employment and what the organization and the individual concerned have done in the past. If there is a mobility clause, for example enabling Hold Your Horses to relocate staff to other branches within the same county, and if there had in fact been transfers between branches, then Olivia would have a strong argument that all sales executives should be put in the same pool. It would then follow that there had to be transparent and objective selection criteria applied to all members of the pool.

5.   Remember that statutory disciplinary and dismissal procedures apply to redundancies where there are fewer than 20 dismissals.

See also Chapter 4.

? Question

You are the HR manager of Premi Air, a manufacturer of air conditioning equipment. Reg is a 67-year-old employee with six months' service. Basil is an agency worker who has also been with you about six months. Both have signed terms and conditions which include a confidentiality clause. Reg and Basil are working together on a piece of equipment when they both receive an electric shock. The incident is reviewed in detail by the technical team and changes are made to the manufacturing process, which will ensure that the incident cannot recur. Reg and Basil are, however, still not satisfied, and demand that 'more should be done'. When Premi Air gives the response that the problem has been completely resolved, and that no further action will or can be taken, Reg and Basil write a joint letter to the local newspaper. A story appears on page 3 under the large headline 'Premi Air Staff in Shock Horror Drama' and in the body of the article Reg and Basil continue to insist that 'more should be done' to protect staff. Your MD is livid and demands that Reg is sacked, and Basil's agency told to take him back immediately.

What issues arise here?

Solution

The Public Interest Disclosure Act was passed in 1998 to make it easier for employees to 'blow the whistle' on their employers, and the Act followed some high-profile cases in which employees were too scared to disclose safety defects at work. The following issues arise in this question:

1. Reg can bring a claim, even though he is 67, as there is no upper age limit on bringing unfair dismissal claims. There is no qualifying period of service, so although Reg has been with you just a short time, he is still able to bring a claim. The Act applies to all workers, not just employees, and so although Basil is an agency worker, he can also bring a claim. Remedies for employees and workers are dealt with below.

2. It may be automatically unfair to dismiss Reg as a result of his making a disclosure which is both 'protected' and a 'qualifying disclosure'. A qualifying disclosure arises if (amongst others) a criminal offence, a failure to comply with a legal obligation, or the endangering of an individual's health and safety has occurred, is occurring, or is likely to occur.

3. For a qualifying disclosure to come within the whistle-blowing legislation it also has to be 'protected'. To be protected, the employee/worker has to act in good faith and have reasonable grounds for believing that the disclosure he makes is a protected disclosure. So if, for example, the employee is motivated by spite or malice, disclosure will not be protected. Or, if the employer has clearly or demonstrably remedied any problem, it is not 'likely to occur'.

4. There are effectively three levels of disclosure and, to be 'protected', a disclosure has to be made in accordance with one of the prescribed methods. First, the Act is worded in such a way as to encourage disclosure within the workplace. Second, the disclosure can be to a list of 'prescribed persons' which includes mainly public bodies such as the Audit Commission, HM Revenue and Customs, Health & Safety Executive, and so forth. Third, there may be external disclosures, but more stringent rules apply to these. The worker must previously have made a disclosure of substantially the same information either to his employer or to a prescribed person, or at the time of the disclosure the worker must believe that he will be subject to a detriment by raising the concern with his employer or a prescribed person, or he must believe that evidence will be concealed or destroyed. In considering whether a disclosure to a third party is a protected disclosure, Tribunals will consider the identity of the person to whom the disclosure is made, the seriousness of the alleged failure, whether it is likely to recur, whether the employee has breached a contractual confidentiality clause, and other factors.

5. If the disclosure is made to a newspaper and relates to a relevant failure which is not particularly serious and is unlikely to be repeated, the worker will have an uphill struggle trying to convince a Tribunal that it was reasonable to act in the way that he did. In the circumstances of this question, we believe it unlikely that Reg and Basil will be able to establish that they have made a qualifying disclosure by contacting a local newspaper.

6. Should, however, a Tribunal find that there has been a qualifying disclosure, and Reg is dismissed as a result, the dismissal will be automatically unfair. It is also important to note that the upper compensation limit of £58,400 does not apply in a whistle-blowing case. In *Fernandes* v. *Netcom* (2000), an accountant who was dismissed after blowing the whistle against his managing director by informing the board of the parent company about fraudulent expenses claims was awarded £293,441 by Reading Employment Tribunal, almost six times the maximum that the Tribunal could have awarded under normal rules. This is because, in addition to a loss of earnings award, in a severe whistle-blowing case there is likely to be a substantial award for injury to feelings and aggravated damages, for example where an employee has exposed a serious risk to public health and safety.

Statutory disciplinary procedures apply here, so if they are not followed any award might be increased by between 10 and 50%.

Basil is an agency worker and so cannot be unfairly dismissed, as unfair dismissal protection applies only to employees. However, following *Dacas* v. *Brook Street Bureau* (2004) and *Cable & Wireless Plc* v. *Muscat* (2006), it is possible that a Tribunal will hold that there is an implied contract of employment between Premi Air and Basil, so that Basil can bring a claim for unfair dismissal. Employees do not need to have 12 months' continuous employment in order to claim unfair dismissal for making a protected disclosure. Even if Basil is not viewed as an 'employee', an agency worker can claim detriment under the whistle-blowing rules, and could also receive an injury to feelings award if his or her contract is terminated as a result of making a qualifying disclosure. The potential financial exposure for Premi Air in respect of Basil, the agency worker, is in fact the same as for Reg, the employee.

However, we do not feel in this case that Reg and Basil will have the benefit of the protection of the whistle-blowing legislation, and so we fall back on general principles. Basil's agency contract can be terminated forthwith, subject only to the slight risk (above) that he could be deemed to be an employee. In respect of Reg, as he has less than 12 months' service he does not qualify for unfair dismissal protection.

7. If Reg had over 12 months' service, and so qualifies for unfair dismissal, a disciplinary meeting should be convened and Reg will be required to answer the charge that he has breached his duty of confidentiality, and brought the employer into disrepute. Whether a Tribunal would regard that as a fair reason to dismiss, and that the employer was fair and reasonable in all the circumstances, is a finely balanced point. On the one hand the company can issue a rebuttal, and no long-term harm to its reputation may result, but on the other hand the Tribunal might take the view that going to the press in such circumstances severely damaged the duty of mutual trust and confidence, as well as harming the reputation of the company unjustifiably.

8. It is recommended that all organizations have a whistle-blowing policy which sets out relevant 'prescribed persons'. This makes it less likely that an external disclosure will be made.

Question

Gerard is employed as a health and safety officer for a multi-site manufacturing company, Easimold, travelling the country to fulfil his role. He is on a 15-month fixed-term contract (which does not contain an early termination clause) due to be revised once the site managers have all received the necessary H & S training to meet the company standard.

Gerard is a keen footballer and halfway through the contract he sustains a serious leg injury one Sunday morning, when tackling a particularly aggressive opponent. The injury means that he will be unable to drive his car for three months. He is surprised to receive a letter from Easimold, stating that his contract is being terminated with immediate effect and that he will no longer be required to work for the company.

What claim does Gerard have against the company, if any?

Solution

1. Breach of contract. In the absence of an early termination clause Gerard could claim damages for the unexpired balance of his 15-month term. The company could possibly counter this claim on the grounds that the contract has been frustrated by Gerard's inability to drive, which is an essential part of his duties,

but it is generally quite difficult to persuade a court or tribunal that a contract has been frustrated.

2. Unfair dismissal. Unlikely, as Gerard does not have 12 months' continuous service. Under the Employment Rights Act (1996), certain reasons for dismissal are automatically unfair. A dismissal that relates to a health and safety issue is one category of automatically unfair dismissal. In this case, although Gerard is employed on health and safety duties, there is nothing to indicate that his dismissal was in any way connected with those duties.

3. Disability discrimination. Again unlikely, unless Gerard is able to demonstrate that his leg injury amounts to a disability under the Disability Discrimination Act (DDA) (1995). For this to apply it would have to have a serious impact on his ability to carry out day-to-day activities and either have lasted or be likely to last for 12 months.

4. Possible breach of the Fixed Term Employees (Prevention of Less Favourable Treatment) Regulations (2002). These Regulations specify the way in which the abuse of successive fixed-term contracts is to be prevented, the circumstances in which a fixed-term contract is deemed to take effect as a permanent contract and the way in which an employee can enforce their rights in the event that they are treated less favourably.

   The Regulations give fixed-term employees the right in principle not to be treated less favourably than a comparable permanent employee. The comparator would need to be 'engaged in the same or broadly similar work having regard, where relevant, to whether they have a similar level of qualifications and skills...'. If Gerard is in a bespoke role then this may not be easy for him to demonstrate.

   If he does find a comparator then he would have to demonstrate that he had suffered a detriment (dismissal would almost certainly qualify) on the grounds that he was a fixed-term worker (which is much more questionable) and that the treatment concerned was not objectively justified.

   Easimold's treatment of permanent employees who are absent due to sickness for an extended period would be relevant evidence – if the company dismisses everyone who cannot work for more than, say, a month regardless of the type of contract then this would assist Easimold. Conversely if the company has a generous company sick pay scheme which is available only to permanent staff then this would be persuasive evidence in Gerard's favour.

   If Gerard was successful in bringing a claim under the Regulations then the Employment Tribunal may award 'just and equitable' compensation to take account of the employee's losses and expenses (but not injury to feelings) subject to the employee's duty to mitigate.

Question

You employ a technician who is likely to be convicted of drink driving next month. His contract states that 'it is a condition of employment that the Employee has and keeps a current driving licence. If the Employee is disqualified from driving for any period the Company reserves the right to dismiss the Employee'. He is a company car driver and you want to dismiss him.

On what grounds can he be dismissed? Do you need to do a full disciplinary hearing? Do you have to pay him notice?

Solution

It is important to remember that although an employee may be in breach of contract, that does not automatically mean it is fair to dismiss him: unfair dismissal focuses on the reasonableness of the employer's decision to dismiss.

If the employee needs his car to carry out his job, and cannot fulfil his employment contract without driving, and thus without a driving licence, it would be unlawful for you to continue to employ him as a driver. You would be in breach of the Road Traffic Act (1991). One of the potentially fair reasons for dismissal is 'breach of an enactment', and thus a dismissal in this circumstance would fall under that category. However, as with any dismissal, it has to be fair and reasonable in all the circumstances, and therefore, rather than dismissing immediately, you need to look at either an alternative way of him performing his existing job, or him undertaking alternative employment for the duration of the ban. If you conclude that neither is workable, then it may be fair to dismiss the employee.

You will also need to ensure that you follow the statutory Disciplinary and Dismissal Procedure (DDP). Under normal unfair dismissal procedures, in a clear-cut case like this, it may be possible to take some short cuts in the process, and perhaps not to have a full disciplinary hearing. However, the DDP is mandatory, so it is necessary to hold meetings and follow the 3-step DDP process, otherwise you will have an automatically unfair dismissal on your hands, no matter how strong your underlying case.

The employee is in breach of contract, which could be considered gross misconduct, meaning that arguably you would not have to pay notice. But most employers would find that a bit harsh, so it is probably appropriate to pay notice.

Question

Jasmine is employed as a secretary for a company specializing in lighting sales. She has worked for them for four years, initially as secretary for the finance director.

In the past 18 months, her job has grown to involve facilities management (FM) and she now finds herself arranging meetings with the cleaning company and calling in the air conditioning supplier to sort out problems. She attended a short course on facilities management to help her in this role. One reason for the shift in focus from secretarial to FM is due to the reduced activity of the finance director at the sales office, but also because there was no one fulfilling the FM role.

The finance director is now moving to the head office in London, following a restructure, and Jasmine has been informed that she will now perform the role of facilities supervisor, reporting to the HR manager. Jasmine is unhappy about the 'imposed' change of job and feels unfairly treated. She resigns and claims constructive dismissal.

Does Jasmine have a claim?

Solution

Historically there has been no consultation with Jasmine – the change in role from full-time secretary to part-time secretary and part-time FM seems to have evolved without her being formally asked if she would like to take on this role. However, by attending the FM course and by undertaking the new role without protest she would appear to have accepted the change to her duties.

Things have moved on and it would appear that the role of secretary has now entirely disappeared with the transfer of the finance director to the London office. The attempt to move Jasmine into a full-time FM role is a further contractual change and the company's attempt to impose this change without consent could well be a breach of contract, entitling Jasmine to resign and claim constructive unfair dismissal. However, employees cannot just resign and submit a Tribunal claim. Jasmine has first to raise the matter in writing, following the statutory grievance procedures, otherwise a Tribunal will not allow her claim to go forward.

Assuming Jasmine has followed the grievance procedures, whether or not such a claim will succeed depends on whether or not the Employment Tribunal considers that the contract of employment has been fundamentally breached by the company's actions. This will be a question of fact but the company would seek to defend its actions on the grounds that Jasmine was largely fulfilling this FM role in any event, that the change was more form over substance and could even be viewed as a promotion for Jasmine. There is of course no guarantee that these lines of defence would succeed but Jasmine's case is not clear-cut either.

If Jasmine's claim for constructive unfair dismissal succeeds then all the usual rules concerning compensation for unfair dismissal will apply – that is, the Basic Award calculated in the same way as a Statutory Redundancy Payment (SRP) and the Compensatory Award (reflecting actual losses) up to the current maximum of £60,400. Jasmine will be under a duty to mitigate her losses by seeking other employment.

What should the company have done? If the secretarial role has now disappeared, then it would appear that this is actually a case of redundancy. In these circumstances, Jasmine should have been consulted and offered the full-time FM role as 'suitable alternative employment' or given notice of redundancy. If an offer of suitable alternative employment is unreasonably declined by an employee then he or she may lose his or her right to a redundancy payment (although this should be treated with caution). Generally Jasmine should have been kept informed and asked for her input in finding a solution; for example, in addition to the FM role, are there other secretarial roles that she could apply for? Could she transfer to the London office with the finance director?

? Question

Lynne works part-time as a care assistant at a day nursery. She has been there for four months when she starts complaining that the building is in a poor state of repair; she says that plaster is falling off one of the walls and this could hit a child. She also complains about dodgy wiring. Her boss is fed up with her complaints, and sacks her, saying that since Lynne has only been here four months she cannot claim unfair dismissal.

Is her boss right?

Solution !

The law provides special protection for workers who are dismissed in connection with 'health and safety' matters. Where an employee works somewhere where there are no health and safety representatives or committees, then if an employee is dismissed because he or she brings to the employer's attention, by reasonable means, circumstances which he or she reasonably believe are harmful or potentially harmful, the dismissal is automatically unfair. In such a case there is no qualifying period and anyone dismissed, even after the briefest of employment, can bring an unfair dismissal claim.

When such a claim is heard by the Tribunal, the burden of proof is shifted onto the employee to show that the reason for dismissal was connected with health and safety. In a conventional unfair dismissal claim, where generally speaking the employer will admit that there was a dismissal, it is for the employer to justify the reasonableness. In an automatic unfair dismissal claim such as this, it falls to the employee to prove that he or she was dismissed for the reason stated. If a Tribunal is satisfied that this is the case, that is effectively an end of the matter, and there will follow a finding of automatic unfair dismissal. It is not open to the employer to argue reasonableness.

Question

Ernie works in a corner shop and is employed by Eric. A large new supermarket opened nearby which started to affect trade. Eric was faced with a loss and a possible closure of the shop if costs were not reduced or income increased. Eric asked Ernie to increase his hours so that the shop could have longer opening times, but without any adjustment to salary. He is dismissed without any notice for refusing to accept new terms and conditions.

What claims would Ernie have and what would he have to show to win these claims?

Solution

Ernie would bring a claim for unfair dismissal. First of all, Ernie would have to establish that he has been employed by Eric for one year. Eric will need to establish the reason for the dismissal, which it appears will fall under 'some other substantial reason' owing to Ernie's refusal to accept the new terms and conditions of his longer hours and adjustment in pay. Eric will have to show that there were good business reasons for this change and the Tribunal would look at the motive for the changes, the method used before implementing the changes and the reasonableness of Ernie refusing the changes.

In establishing that there is a sound business reason, Eric will not have to show that the business was on the verge of financial collapse, but just that the changes were necessary. It is not enough for an employer to impose a change in terms and conditions in order to increase their own profit unless there is a business need to do so.

However, the first question for the Tribunal is likely to be whether Eric made any attempt to follow the statutory disciplinary procedures, by informing Ernie in writing of the grounds that have led Eric to consider dismissing Ernie, and then holding a meeting. If this has not been done, the dismissal will be automatically unfair.

If Eric did follow the DDP, this does not mean that the dismissal is fair: the Tribunal will look at the way that Eric tried to implement the changes and whether he discussed with Ernie the reasons that the changes were necessary, allowing Ernie to make any representations about the situation and to see whether Eric made any effort to try to secure Ernie's consent to the changes.

How reasonable was Ernie in refusing the changes? This will be a matter of fact for the Tribunal to decide, but Tribunals do take very seriously any cases that deal with a reduction in an employee's wages, which it ultimately would have done as Ernie would have had to work longer hours for the same pay.

It is unlikely that Ernie's contract would allow him to be dismissed without notice for any reason other than gross misconduct and it is unlikely that a Tribunal would find that his refusal to enter into new terms and conditions would be gross misconduct. Therefore it is likely that Ernie would be successful in an unfair dismissal claim and also a wrongful dismissal claim, as the breach of contract is Eric's refusal to pay his notice payment.

Other issues here include working time – was Ernie working over 48 hours and, if so, had he opted out? Does the new rate of pay exceed the minimum wage?

❓ Question

Bob is a builder and has a fixed-term contract of 12 months. The company does not have any complaints about Bob's work, but the managing director has told you not to renew his contract to ensure that he does not obtain enough continuous employment for a redundancy payment.

Are you entitled just to let Bob's contract lapse at the end of the 12-month period?

Solution

The non-renewal of a fixed-term contract constitutes a dismissal for the purposes of the Employment Rights Act 1996, which means that by the time of his termination Bob will have acquired 12 months' continuous service to be entitled to claim unfair dismissal.

Therefore, the company will have to prove that the non-renewal of the fixed-term contract (that is, the termination) was a fair dismissal. This means proving substantive fairness (one of the five potential fair reasons) and procedural fairness.

If the reason for the dismissal does not fall into these categories, then the dismissal will be unfair. On the face of it, there does not appear to be any fair reason for not renewing the fixed-term contract, apart from the MD not wishing Bob's continuous service to build up. A reason which is usually consistent with fixed-term employees is that the work for which the employee was taken on has lapsed, and so the fair reason would be either some other substantial reason (that the employee was taken on for only 12 months because there would be no work after that) or redundancy.

The Tribunal will still have to be convinced that a fair procedure was followed, and, in ending a fixed-term contract, that would mean notifying Bob a month or so before the contract is about to expire to inform him that the contract is not to be renewed. There would be an obligation on the employer to see if there is any suitable alternative employment, and if there is genuinely none available then the contract would automatically expire. In addition, the statutory Disciplinary and Dismissal Procedure applies to non-renewal of a fixed-term contract, and if this have not been followed, this dismissal will be automatically unfair.

Generally therefore, you could not just allow the fixed-term contract to lapse without having some liability for an unfair dismissal claim.

Under the Fixed Term Employees (Prevention of Less Favourable Treatment) Regulations, which came into effect on 1 October 2002, there is an obligation for employers to inform fixed-term employees of permanent vacancies within the organization, and if this has not been fulfilled then Bob may have a claim under these Regulations.

Note that fixed-term employees cannot now waive their rights to claim statutory redundancy pay, which they are entitled to if they have the requisite continuous service.

However, a cynical employer could avoid unfair dismissal liability by dismissing before the employee has 12 months' service: in *Department of Work and Pensions* v. *Webley* (2005) the DWP had a policy of dismissing employees on fixed-term contracts after 51 weeks. The Court of Appeal held that this was lawful: the employee did not have sufficient service to claim unfair dismissal, and the termination of a fixed-term contract could not itself amount to 'less favourable treatment' under the Fixed Term Employees Prevention of Less Favourable Treatment Regulations.

Question

Greg works in a large car-manufacturing plant as a line manager. He has 27 employees under him, at least half of whom are Asian.

Whilst at a football match two weeks ago, Greg was involved in some trouble and was caught on CCTV throwing a punch at an Asian spectator. The police were involved, and Greg's name appeared in the local paper, although he was not prosecuted on this occasion. Greg maintains that he was provoked, and that he got swept along in the heat of the moment.

One of his work colleagues has formally complained and said that he should have been dismissed owing to this 'brush with the law'. Some of his reportees say they will not work for him.

What do you do?

Solution

Greg was not formally prosecuted by the police. However, even if he had been formally prosecuted, it will not automatically mean that he should be dismissed from his employment. The ACAS Code of Conduct, in dealing with employees' criminal conduct, states that 'the main consideration should be whether the offence, or alleged offence, is one that makes the employee unsuitable for their type of work'. If there is a prosecution against an employee, an employer must look at what it is for and how relevant that is to his employment. Offences of dishonesty, which occur outside the workplace, may often lead to a dismissal, as honesty is a fundamental part of the relationship and the term of trust and confidence between employer and employee. There would certainly therefore be no automatic dismissal because he has had a 'brush with the law'.

However, if Greg is a line manager, then there is a question of whether his behaviour outside the workplace affects his authority and status within the workplace. This is especially significant where the allegations against him involved a racial element and many of his work colleagues and reportees are Asian.

The first practical step to take would be to talk to Greg and understand exactly what his side of the story is. Although the conduct occurred outside the workplace, it may be seen to bring the company into disrepute (the company's name may have been mentioned in the local newspaper) and it may be that disciplinary action against Greg should be taken.

Regardless of this step, the reportees who say they will not work for Greg should all be spoken to, to see if any action can be taken apart from either Greg's dismissal or their resignation. The employer can also treat a refusal by other employees to work with someone as misconduct, and follow disciplinary procedures against those employees. Where one person or a number of people are refusing to work with another colleague owing to his or her conduct, then Greg could be dismissed for some other substantial reason and as long as a fair procedure has been followed, an unfair dismissal claim can be resisted. In any event, employers must always ensure they follow the statutory disciplinary and grievance procedures.

Question

Jane is accused of accessing an internet site which is prohibited by the company policy. Jane says that she has not seen the policy because she was ill the day it was distributed and signed by other employees. She also says that other employees access the same kind of sites and no action is ever taken against them.

What do you do?

Solution

Apparently more employees are dismissed for e-mail and/or internet abuse than for any other type of misconduct.

It is essential, however, that if an employee is to be disciplined and especially dismissed for such abuse, there is a policy which clearly prohibits certain behaviour.

In *Dunn* v. *IBM United Kingdom Ltd* (1998), Dunn was dismissed for gross misconduct for misusing company assets by accessing pornography and other non-business-related material via the internet. Dunn successfully claimed unfair dismissal. One of the main reasons was that although the employee had admitted being responsible for printouts of downloaded pictures found in the print room, he had no appreciation that this would lead to dismissal because there was no policy prohibiting his actions. The dismissal for gross misconduct was not therefore a reasonable response.

Therefore, any action that can be taken by Jane's employer in these circumstances depends on the chances of Jane knowing that the internet site, which she visited, was a forbidden site. Was the policy circulated only on the day that Jane was absent? Many employers have such policies in handbooks, which are readily available to all employees, or on the company intranet. If Jane has not seen the policy it is unlikely that she can be dismissed for gross misconduct, unless the site that she visited can lead to criminal charges.

Even if Jane has seen the policy, if the policy has not been enforced by the company and other employees regularly breach it without any action being taken against them, it would be difficult to dismiss Jane fairly for gross misconduct. A Tribunal would probably find that this was not a reasonable response, as Jane did not have proper warning that she would be dismissed because no one else followed the policy.

Depending on the findings after a thorough investigation into the allegations and whether other employees follow the company's policy, it would probably be best to give Jane a written warning explaining that a further breach of the policy will probably lead to summary dismissal.

It is advisable that she is required now to sign a copy of the policy. It is also useful to remind employees of the company's policy on computer use via messages on the computer, such as when employees sign on in the morning.

Question

Jane is given a written warning, even though under the company policy her actions would amount to gross misconduct. Two weeks later your office is being rearranged and behind a filing cabinet you find a copy of the company computer policy signed by Jane.

Are you entitled to take any action, and if so, what?

Solution

An employer can arrange for a disciplinary issue to be heard again, where further evidence comes to light. Jane should be told what new evidence has been uncovered and told when a new disciplinary hearing will take place. Although it may seem to be a straightforward case at the outset, Jane may have an explanation for the finding of her signed policy and an investigation may be necessary. Jane should be warned at the outset that the disciplinary hearing could lead to her dismissal.

Although the employer still has the problem that other employees may also be in breach of the company policy and this is not enforced, there is now a new allegation against Jane, which is dishonesty. If she blatantly lied about signing the computer policy, then this would be an act of gross misconduct sufficient to lead to her dismissal.

If Jane says that she does not remember signing the policy then she can still be dismissed for gross misconduct if the employer has an honest belief that the misconduct existed, that is, she lied about not signing the policy.

Question

Cappercaille Publishing deal with the reproduction of sheet music on the web. Any music can be printed off for a fee, by anyone with a valid credit card and access to the internet. Recently, several complaints have been received from the artists, stating that they have not been paid their share for the reproduction of their work, although their records show that their music has in fact been downloaded.

The two employees whose job it is to manage these payments, Terry and Leslie, have assured you that they are processing the payments correctly, but you suspect either one or both of them of somehow misappropriating the revenue owed to your clients. You are certain that one or other of them is guilty of theft, but you are not sure which one.

Can you discipline them?

Solution

Before taking any disciplinary action against anyone in these circumstances, you would need to ensure that there is some substance to the complaints being made and therefore a full investigation would need to be carried out. The investigation would also look at whether there are any other explanations for why artists are not receiving their share of revenue for the reproduction of their work. If at the end of the investigation it does appear that either Terry or Leslie is guilty and it is not possible to distinguish which one of them it is, then it is possible to dismiss them both.

The offence itself is one of gross misconduct as it is one of theft, and although this will leave the publishing company in a slight difficulty in having to replace them both at the same time, it would be extremely difficult to justify dismissing only one of them on the basis that the company cannot ascertain which individual is responsible. Where one is dismissed and the other is not, there could be a successful unfair dismissal claim. The case authority for this is *Frames Snooker Centre* v. *Boyce* (1992), where it was held by the Employment Appeal Tribunal:

> as a general rule, if the circumstances of the members of the group in relation to the relevant offence are similar it is likely to be unreasonable for the employer to dismiss one or more members of the group and not others, and those dismissed will thus succeed in a claim for unfair dismissal. But if the employer is able to show that he has solid and sensible grounds (which do not have to be related to the relevant offence) for differentiating between members of the group and not dismissing one or more of them, that will not of itself render the dismissal of the remainder unfair.

In the Frames Snooker Centre case there were three managers of a snooker centre, one of those being the daughter of the proprietor. Three burglaries took place and after investigations the police formed the view that each burglary was an inside job. The suspects were the managers as they all had keys to the snooker centre, knew the code number of the combination safe lock and had an intimate knowledge of the premises. After the third burglary the proprietor felt that he had no alternative but to dismiss two of the managers but he did not dismiss his daughter because he had faith in her honesty and evidence that she had placed money in the safe that day. Although the original Industrial Tribunal upheld one of the manager's complaints for unfair dismissal, the Employment Appeal Tribunal overturned it.

Question

Terence and Philip have just been investigated for breaching the alcohol and drugs policy, both getting horrendously drunk at a work function, even though no harm was done. They currently both have a written warning and the next stage of the disciplinary procedure is a final written warning before dismissal with notice. Their line manager wants to give Terence a final warning, but dismiss Philip.

What is your advice?

Solution

This question with regard to giving different employees different disciplinary sanctions if they are guilty of an identical offence brings up a number of issues which could make a great deal of difference to the outcome. If Philip is dismissed and he brings a claim for unfair dismissal, he will allege that he should not have been dismissed for the offence and the Tribunal will have to decide on a factual basis whether or not the employer's dismissal was 'within the band of reasonable responses'. There would certainly be a very strong argument for a Tribunal to find that it is not within the band of reasonable responses to dismiss one employee where the other has been given a final written warning and there is no reason for distinguishing between them. Length of service and previous disciplinary records have to be considered.

Of course, there may also be other issues that come to light. For example, if Philip claimed that he had been discriminated against on the basis of any of the grounds of unlawful discrimination then he would put forward an argument to the Tribunal that the only reason that he was given a more severe penalty than Terence was due to his race, sex, disability, sexual orientation, religion or age. Once Philip has raised some evidence from which an inference of discrimination could be drawn, the burden of proof shifts to the employer to show that race etc played no part whatsoever in the decision to dismiss Philip but not Terence.

The advice to the manager is that he must be consistent and either dismiss them both (assuming that this is a reasonable penalty) or give them both a final written warning, unless there is a very clear justification for treating Philip more severely.

? Question

You have an employee who is signed off sick, and you have received a tip-off that he is working for another employer. His manager appointed a private investigator to follow the employee and to make a secret video tape of him. The investigator obtained some slightly fuzzy footage, on one occasion, of the employee dropping off a van at a transport company. The manager held a disciplinary based on that evidence. The employee said that

a) he was only dropping of a van for a friend and was not working, and that in doing so was not in conflict with his sickness;
b) secretly videoing him in this way was in breach of his human rights; and
c) the company is also in breach of the Data Protection Act (1998).

Despite these issues, the manager went ahead and dismissed him and you are now hearing the Appeal. The same points have cropped up again. How do you deal with the Appeal?

Solution

1. The first point to be concerned about is that the manager appears to have been both the investigator and the decision maker of the disciplinary. Potentially the whole process is fatally flawed as a result. If a manager has been involved in dealing with the tip-off, briefing a private investigator and generally dealing with an investigation, it is essential that he passes the matter to a different, independent manager who will then conduct the disciplinary hearing. Faced with this situation, at the appeal stage you will have to ensure that you conduct a re-hearing, which means that you go through all of the evidence again, treating it as a full disciplinary hearing, rather than an appeal against an existing decision.

2. At a practical level, the manager has proceeded on the basis of some fairly weak evidence. Experience shows that if an employee is caught out doing something once, he can often construct some kind of plausible excuse. Rather than rushing in to the disciplinary, it would have been better to ask the enquiry agent to continue investigations and see if he can spot the employee working on two or more occasions. That will be far harder for him to answer.

3. Employees and, where appropriate, their union representatives, will often make unspecific wide ranging allegations such as 'breach of human rights', 'breach of Data Protection Act'. The first step to take if such an allegation is made is to ask the employee or the representative to specify with precision which parts of which legislation it is being alleged have been breached, and how.

4. The Human Rights Act (1998) has direct applicability to the public sector only. However, an Employment Tribunal is in the public sector. If a Tribunal believes that evidence has been obtained in a manner which breaches the Human Rights Act, the Tribunal may hold itself bound under the Human Rights Act to disregard that evidence. In this case, were the Tribunal to disregard the video evidence, the whole disciplinary case would fall away, leaving the employer with no defence. However, that is very unlikely as a number of cases over the last few years have demonstrated that Tribunals are willing to accept covertly obtained recordings or videos where the employer is acting proportionately and investigating wrongdoing such as, in this case, a fraudulent claim for sick pay.

   There is unlikely to be any breach of the Data Protection Act in this case, as the data is gathered as part of the investigation, is legitimately obtained and has been processed properly through the disciplinary procedure.

So, in terms of dealing with the appeal, you should, as stated above, treat this as a full re-hearing, and go through all the evidence. Reject the complaints about the video evidence and look at that. You have to be satisfied as to the employee's guilt on the basis of a reasonable belief following an adequate investigation. You do not need absolute proof – the 'beyond reasonable doubt' test applies only to criminal cases. Here, you might be inclined to think that the investigation was inadequate, in which case you should consider whether there is anything that can be done, now, to enhance that investigation. If you think more investigation is needed, you should adjourn the appeal hearing, and ask someone else to carry out further investigations and report to you in due course. For example, has anyone contacted the owner of the business at which the employee was seen allegedly working? As soon as you think there is adequate information, you can reconvene the appeal, having given the employee the opportunity to respond to any new evidence, and make a decision.

Question

One of your secretaries, Barbara, has shown herself to be lazy and incompetent. She has been with you for five years and the issue has not been properly addressed throughout that time. The MD says that he wants her out and it must happen within a week.

What can you do to minimize the risks?

Solution

Barbara has never been advised that there were concerns about her performance. As such the issues have not been recorded at any appraisals and Barbara has never been put on a performance improvement plan. To now dismiss Barbara without following any kind of procedures will undoubtedly be unfair.

If the company also fails to follow the statutory dismissal procedures the dismissal will be automatically unfair and this would lead the Employment Tribunal to increase any award by between 10–50 per cent.

In order for a dismissal to be fair, you must consider two aspects. First, ensure you comply with the usual 'reasonableness' principles and second, you need to comply with the statutory dismissal procedures. The statutory dismissal procedure is as follows:

Step 1   Write to the employee notifying them of the allegations against them and the basis of the allegations and invite them to a meeting to discuss the matter.

Step 2   Hold a meeting to discuss the allegations – at which the employee has the right to be accompanied – and notify the employee of the decision and of the right to appeal. (Note: The Step 2 meeting should only go ahead after the employee has had a 'reasonable opportunity' to consider their response to the allegations.)

Step 3   If the employee wishes to appeal, hold an appeal meeting at which the employee has the right to be accompanied – and inform the employee of the final decision.

If it is necessary to comply with the MD's instruction to get her out within a week, you probably have just about enough time to comply with the statutory dismissal procedure. (The appeal does not have to happen within the week – that can be later). This will stop the dismissal being automatically unfair but the timescale means that it is highly unlikely that the dismissal will be fair under the usual 'reasonableness' principles.

The best way to minimize the risks to the company would be to offer Barbara a compromise agreement. The procedure for this is as follows:

• You should give Barbara the 'Step 1' letter, notifying her of the allegations and inviting her to a meeting to discuss the matter. You (or, preferably, someone else in the organization) will then have an 'off the record' discussion with Barbara and explain that as an alternative to going through the disciplinary procedure the company is offering an ex gratia payment under a compromise agreement.
• If Barbara is interested in this option, she will seek legal advice and hopefully sign the compromise agreement.
• If she refuses or drags her feet about the terms of the compromise agreement, you will then proceed to have the 'Step 2' meeting and continue with the statutory dismissal procedures so that the dismissal is not automatically unfair.

By giving her the 'Step 1' letter prior to the 'without prejudice' discussion the Company will:

• have a valid dispute to discuss with Barbara 'off the record';
• show Barbara's legal advisor that the company is intending to follow a fair disciplinary procedure;
• retain an 'escape route' if Barbara refuses to sign the compromise agreement.

This letter is therefore an important safeguard.

If the company dismisses Barbara without giving her any warnings then, although the dismissal will not be automatically unfair (having complied with the statutory procedures), it is likely that the company will still have to defend a 'normal' unfair dismissal claim based on the company's unreasonable actions in dismissing her without warnings or following a fair procedure overall.

The way to avoid or reduce the risk of an unfair dismissal claim is to ensure that the dismissal is fair. You would need to give Barbara warnings and monitor and review her performance. If there is insufficient improvement, you would be entitled to dismiss Barbara on conduct and/or capability grounds. This procedure would obviously take much longer but would significantly reduce the company's exposure to a claim and, in any event, would not prevent you from seeking to reach a compromise with Barbara along the way.

With regard to the amount to offer Barbara in the agreement, as a secretary she is likely to be in a position to mitigate her loss fairly quickly. Therefore a payment of about three months' salary would be a reasonable offer, but if she argues for a lot more you may need to obtain information about alternative vacancies in the locality to demonstrate that she had not taken all reasonable steps to mitigate her loss.

Question

You have just realized that Oleg has 51 weeks' continuous service. You never intended to keep him on permanently and you now need to get rid of him today before his one year's service gives him the right to claim unfair dismissal.

Can you dismiss him now and get away with it?

Solution

If you communicate instant dismissal or dismissal with one week's notice to Oleg today and today is the last day of the 51st week of continuous employment, you will not face an unfair dismissal claim unless that claim is for one of the automatically unfair reasons that do not require one year's continuous service. It may also be possible for Oleg to claim that his dismissal was unlawful discrimination on grounds of sex, race, disability etc as there is no requirement of continuous employment for these claims.

However, if today is the first day of the 52nd week and you dismiss Oleg with or without notice, you are too late!

This is because employees with service of less than one year are entitled to one week's statutory notice and the Employment Rights Act 1996 specifies that Employment Tribunals include the statutory (note: not contractual) notice period when deciding if an employee 'has been continuously employed for a period of not less one year ending with the effective date of termination' in relation to unfair dismissal eligibility.

Rather confusingly, this rule does not apply in deciding whether Oleg would be entitled to a Basic Award. For these purposes, if Oleg did have a claim, he would have less than one year's continuous employment and would only be entitled to claim compensation, but no Basic Award.

Question

You have a pool of cars that employees can use for work purposes. Contrary to your strict rules on the use of these cars, Moira, who has worked with you for two years, used a pool car to drive all of her friends to a nightclub on Saturday night. She crashed the car, drove the car back to the car park and denied all knowledge of it. A full investigation was carried out, at the end of which it was fairly obvious that Moira was the guilty party. Moira's manager sent the evidence to Moira, after which Moira wrote back admitting it and apologizing for all the trouble she'd caused and saying she 'would resign if that's what you want'. Moira's manager wrote back informing Moira that she was dismissed.

Moira has now appealed. What do you do?

Solution

As it stands at the moment, this dismissal will be automatically unfair, as the employer has failed to follow the statutory disciplinary procedures. It is necessary, in accordance with the Employment Act 2002 (Dispute Resolution) Regulations 2004, to have a hearing before any decision is made as to whether to dismiss. The employee may be allowed to give an explanation during the investigative stage but, obviously, there is a risk that not all matters will have been put to the employee where, for instance, the investigation has not been completed. Ensure that at least one formal meeting takes place with the employee before dismissal/disciplinary action is taken or a decision is taken on a grievance that has been raised. The employee has a right to be accompanied, and a right of appeal.

You can't 'un-dismiss' someone. Once they have been served with unambiguous notice of dismissal, you cannot later retract the termination without their consent. Therefore, the only thing you can do to avoid an unfair dismissal finding is offer Moira the chance to be reinstated so you can go through a fair dismissal procedure.

In this case, if Moira does bring an Employment Tribunal claim you would have a strong argument for saying that she would have been dismissed in any event (the so-called 'Polkey' argument) and that her own conduct contributed to the dismissal, so her compensation should be minimal.

However, the Tribunal is almost bound to offer a Basic Award for unfair dismissal and to increase the Compensatory Award by at least 10 per cent for the failure to follow the DDP.

Managers need to be aware that – even in the most clear-cut cases – they still have to follow the basic statutory disciplinary procedure before dismissing.

Chapter 11

Miscellaneous

❓ Question

A personnel officer resigned from his post to take up a new position. The new job was offered subject to a suitable reference from the personnel officer's last employer. When asked, the employer explained it was company policy not to give references. The offer from the new employer was withdrawn as a result, leaving the personnel officer out of work.

Does the personnel officer have any rights of compensation from his last employer?

Solution ❗

An employer is not obliged to provide a reference, and will only be liable for not doing so if: having promised (by contract or otherwise) to provide a reference he now refuses to do; or the reason for not giving the reference is based on discriminatory grounds (sex, race, disability, sexual orientation, religious belief and age.) If neither of these reasons applies in this case, the company will have no liability in respect of the personnel officer losing the job.

With regards to references generally, if a reference is given, certain obligations and liabilities will arise. The ex-employer will be under a duty to ensure that the reference is true, accurate and fair and does not give a misleading impression. Otherwise it may face a claim in negligence by the ex-employee and the new employer. It will face an action for libel only if it knows the content of the reference to be untrue.

The Data Protection Act 1998 is also a consideration to bear in mind when deciding whether or not to give a reference. The 1998 Act gives wider access rights to individuals about whom information is held, although Schedule 7 to the Act sets out a number of exceptions. One exception is that an individual is not entitled to have access to any reference given, or to be given, in confidence by his or her employer if the reference is given for the purposes of the education, training or employment of the individual; the appointment of the individual to any office; or the provision by the individual of any service.

However, the individual will still be able to apply to the new employer for a copy of the reference as the exception does not cover references held by third parties, that is, the new employer. That being said, if disclosure of the reference would necessarily identify the author (who is himself or herself a data subject), the reference cannot be disclosed without that author's consent. If the author refuses to give his or her consent, the new employer would have to decide whether the benefit of the disclosure outweighs the duty of confidentiality.

Question

Ten months ago, Ursula was regraded. You have just discovered that her salary was increased by two grades, not by the one grade it should have been.

How do you set about recovering the money?

Solution

The provisions in Part II of the Employment Rights Act 1996 prohibiting deductions from wages without specific statutory or contractual authority or the employee's express written consent do not apply where 'the purpose of the deduction is the reimbursement of the employer in respect of [...] an overpayment of wages'. At first sight, therefore, you can simply deduct the money from Ursula's next pay packet/s without even seeking, let alone obtaining, her agreement. That may not, however, be the wisest course.

For the above to apply, the employer must have a legal right to recoup the money. Under the general law, the right to recoup a payment which has mistakenly been made depends on the nature of the mistake. A payment made under a 'mistake of law' is not recoverable. A mistake of law occurs when the payer genuinely, but erroneously, believes that the payee is legally entitled to the money. A payment made under a 'mistake of fact' – which in practice covers any other error – is, in principle, recoverable; but a court may still refuse to order its repayment if:

- the payer has represented to the payee that the money is his or hers; and
- the payee, relying on that representation, has changed his or her position – which essentially means spent the money – and the payee is in no way to blame for the mistake;
- the payee was acting in good faith throughout.

It is by no means self-evident from the facts stated here that, were you to sue Ursula for the return of the money or were you to make a deduction and Ursula were to sue you for the return of the deducted amount, you would win. Any case would raise issues about how the mistake occurred; whether Ursula genuinely and reasonably believed (because you had been paying it regularly for 10 months) she was entitled to the extra money, and whether her spending pattern had altered to reflect such a belief.

Bearing this in mind, and also the likelihood that the sudden deduction of the full amount from Ursula's next pay packet/s would almost certainly cause her cash flow problems, it may be preferable to discuss the matter with her and to hope to reach some agreed programme of repayments. It is important to remember that, from Ursula's point of view, she will not only be facing the prospect of repaying past overpayments but also of having to do that out of a diminished income: the rate she has been used to receiving over the last 10 months will, now that the mistake has been discovered, anyway be reduced. As a matter of psychology, not law, she will probably be much less likely to contemplate or take legal action if the position is explained to her and her cooperation sought in finding a sympathetic method of resolving the problem. And, as a matter of law, you will not – by taking such an approach – be altering such rights as you have to make deduction/s without Ursula's agreement if, in such discussions, she proves intransigent.

Question

You are negotiating terms of a compromise agreement and the outgoing employee is hoping to wrap up her notice pay, statutory redundancy pay and accrued holiday entitlement into a tax-free payment.

Can you agree to this?

You have noticed that the employee has no restrictive covenants and you are concerned about the employee taking customers.

Can you now introduce covenants, and what are the taxation implications?

Solution !

The starting point is that all payments on termination are taxable. The £30,000 tax-free exemption under Section 401 (and s403) Income Tax (Earnings and Pensions) Act 2003 (ITEPA) is an exemption where a payment is not otherwise chargeable to tax.

If a payment is made pursuant to a contractual entitlement it is taxable under s62 ITEPA. This is the standard provision under which income tax is chargeable.

If a contract has a clause to the effect 'we reserve the right to pay in lieu of notice', known as a PILON clause, then any payments under that clause, ie when the employee is in fact paid in lieu of notice, are taxed. By contrast, if there is no such clause the employer is technically in breach of contract if it pays in lieu of notice without a contractual right to do so. The payment is therefore damages for breach of contract, which is not taxable.

S401 taxes payments not covered by s62. Specifically s401(1)(a) deals with payments on termination, for example redundancy (both statutory and contractual), retirement, dismissal, resignation etc. Tax is levied only to the extent that such payments, in total, exceed £30,000.

Therefore, if an employee receives a payment in lieu of notice pursuant to a PILON clause in his or her contract of employment as part of a settlement deal under a compromise agreement, the payment will be fully taxable. If there is no PILON clause s62 will generally not apply and therefore the £30,000 exemption should apply. Statutory and contractual redundancy payments are not taxed under s62 but do form part of the £30,000 exemption. Paid holidays are a contractual entitlement and therefore s62 will apply to this part of the payment, so both must be taxed.

Tax may be deducted on the excess over £30,000 at basic rate, currently 22 per cent. The employee may have a further tax demand later, depending on his or her circumstances in the rest of the current tax year. So it is important to obtain a tax indemnity if tax is deducted at basic rate.

It is possible to introduce restrictive covenants on termination, but clearly the employee may not be inclined to agree to them. If a payment is made in return for covenants, that payment is fully taxable. If there are other tax-free elements of the package, the payment for the covenants might taint the whole deal, rendering it all taxable. So it is recommended to split the payments, allocating a taxable amount to the covenant, and keeping the tax-free element separate.

? Question

Semirah works as a systems trainer for a pharmaceutical company and has been employed for nine years. She moved into the systems role eight months ago and during this time has taken five weeks off sick – usually in blocks of four days. She has struggled to learn the new role but has found little support from the small, over-stretched team in which she works.

Her line manager has changed twice in this period and little attention has been paid to either the absence or Semirah's performance. Her latest manager is Tom.

She is surprised, therefore, to be told at her appraisal interview that she is being issued with a formal verbal warning for poor performance and attendance. She leaves the office, dismayed. The following day, her line manager receives a doctor's certificate, signing Semirah off work for two weeks with depression. Semirah subsequently resigns.

What claims does Semirah have, if any, against the company?

Solution

1. Constructive unfair dismissal. However, in order to succeed in this claim Semirah must show that her employer's conduct constituted a breach of a fundamental term in her contract (including the implied term of trust and confidence) or that it demonstrated an intention on the employer's part no longer to be bound by the terms of the contract. Even if she can point to a specific breach of a term – for example, that warnings should only be given within the context of a formal disciplinary process and not as part of the appraisal process – the question facing the Tribunal is likely to be one of degree rather than principle. Was any such breach really serious enough to entitle her to resign? Given the essentially procedural nature of the employer's failing, she may have difficulty convincing the Tribunal of that.

    She would have to demonstrate not just that the employer had acted unreasonably but that it had acted so unreasonably that she really had little choice other than to leave. She will not be able to bring her complaint before a Tribunal unless she has first raised the matter in writing with the employer, in accordance with the statutory grievance procedures.

2. Failure to be accompanied at a disciplinary hearing. Under Section 10 of the Employment Relations Act 1999, all employees have the right to be accompanied by a colleague or trade union official

(whether or not the union is recognized by the employer) at any disciplinary or grievance hearing. The penalty is a maximum of two weeks' pay. A disciplinary hearing is any hearing which could result in 'the administration of a formal warning to a worker'. Recent case law has held that a verbal warning can constitute a 'formal' warning if it forms part of the employer's disciplinary procedure or would be recorded on the employee's file. In this case the company has started with an appraisal meeting but then turned it into a disciplinary meeting without warning the employee of this or informing her of her right to be accompanied, so there is likely to be a technical breach and liability under this head.

3.   Discrimination. Semirah would need to consider whether the treatment she has received is a detriment to which she has been subject on the grounds of her race, sex, disability, religion or sexual orientation, or, from October 2006, age. Is Semirah's illness a disability under the Disability Discrimination Act (DDA)? Has Tom perhaps failed to discipline men who have similar periods of absence? Is Semirah of different ethnic origin to others who have not been disciplined in similar circumstances? The revised procedures on the burden of proof may help Semirah here: if she is able to show some facts from which the Tribunal could conclude that there has been discrimination, then it will look to the employer for an explanation.

4.   Stress-related personal injury damages. Semirah has become depressed as a result of Tom's actions – can she claim damages for this? Following the guidance given by the Court of Appeal in *Hatton* v. *Sutherland* (2002), it is unlikely that she will be successful. In order to succeed in this claim it would be necessary to demonstrate both that the company was in breach of its duty of care to Semirah and that the damage she has suffered is a reasonably foreseeable consequence of this breach, in the light of what the employer knew or ought to have known. These hurdles would both seem too high in the circumstances of this case, although everything will depend upon the particular facts.

Question

Two months after his termination date, you receive a letter from an ex-employee telling you that the only reason he resigned was because his line manager bullied him. He says he wants the manager concerned to be 'dealt with'. This employee was always given to exaggeration when he worked for you. He was also quite confrontational and aggressive – you spent many hours in grievance meetings with him during his employment and were delighted when you saw his resignation letter. You find it hard to believe he was bullied by his line manager (or anyone else for that matter).

You don't believe a word of his letter and don't really want to get involved in further confrontational meetings with him, given that he's now left. What do you do?

Solution

Prior to October 2004, you might have sent a quick note thanking him for his letter and leaving it there.

You might have suspected he was building up some sort of constructive dismissal claim against you, but nothing you do after his termination would have much effect on the outcome. In order to win his claim of constructive dismissal, he would have to prove there was some sort of fundamental breach of contract *before* his resignation that caused him to resign in protest. Failing to deal fully with his whingeing letter *after* his resignation might not show you in the most reasonable light but it would have little if any impact on the outcome of his claim.

However, this is arguably a grievance letter and grievances took on an added importance in October 2004 with the introduction of the DDP, which also introduced a new statutory grievance procedure.

Although the procedure itself is fairly simple (Grievance Letter; Meeting; Appeal), the effects of the new procedure on Tribunal claims can be quite considerable: a) employees can be prevented from bringing certain claims (such as discrimination claims and constructive dismissal claims – not dismissal claims as these are covered by the statutory dismissal procedures) before an Employment Tribunal if they have not previously brought the matter to the attention of their employer under a grievance procedure and then waited 28 days; b) if a grievance is brought and an employer fails to deal with it properly, then, if the employee later brings a successful Employment Tribunal claim, their compensation can be increased by up to 50 per cent for the employer's failure to follow the DDP.

As far as the employee is concerned, the effect is not all that disastrous. Employees who have failed to raise grievances will not be barred from bringing the claim altogether; provided they have raised their Tribunal claim or their grievance within the normal time limit for bringing the claim (generally three months) then the time limit for bringing their tribunal claim will be extended by three months. Therefore, the employee will have time to raise the grievance and wait 28 days and then submit their claim and still be within the time limit. Effectively the claim is only delayed.

However, as far as the employer is concerned, failure to follow the DDP after an employee has raised a grievance can have a large and irreversible impact on the amount of compensation that an employee stands to win at Tribunal. This is made all the more problematic by the fact that Tribunals have, since the introduction of the DDP, given a fairly broad interpretation to what constitutes a Grievance Letter.

For example, in one case, an employee who had already resigned and left her employment wrote to her former employer suggesting that she had been badly treated and that she intended to bring a Tribunal claim. The letter did not purport to be a grievance letter. However, the Tribunal in that case ruled that it was a Grievance Letter under the DDP.

In another case, an employee's letter complaining about the manner in which a disciplinary meeting had been held was deemed sufficient to constitute a Grievance Letter, despite the fact that it did not mention the grievance procedure at all. And a woman's letter complaining about the fact that her flexible working request had been turned down (which she wrote at the end of a series of meetings about the request) was deemed to constitute a Grievance Letter.

Therefore, the danger for employers is:

1. Employee writes whingeing letter – or even a whingeing e-mail.
2. Employer responds, but does not act in line with the DDP (does not invite employee to a meeting, allow employee to be accompanied and allow an appeal, etc).
3. Employee raises claim (eg constructive unfair dismissal) and wins.
4. Employee's compensation is increased by between 10 and 50 per cent.

It is not really practicable to treat every single disgruntled employee's letter and e-mail as a Grievance Letter – managers would never do anything but attend grievance meetings! However, it is probably worth responding to all letters and e-mails from employees that raise complaints by asking: 'Would you like this matter to be dealt with through the Grievance Procedure?'

It is also worth remembering that, although employees can bring grievances after they have already left employment, and the DDP does require that they are dealt with, it is possible (provided you get the employee's written consent first) to deal with the matter through the Statutory Modified Grievance Procedure, which only requires you to respond to the grievance in writing and allow an appeal, rather than holding a series of meetings.

? Question

An employee gets a bad appraisal and reacts badly. The following day, she calls her line manager to say she doesn't 'feel like' coming to work. You later get a doctor's certificate signing her off with 'work-related stress'.

Is there anything you can do?

Solution !

Stress is not an illness. However, it is often found on doctors' sick notes, the technical term for which is MED3s, which are – at least on the face of it – evidence that an employee is unfit to attend work and eligible to receive statutory sick pay. Most company sick pay policies are triggered at the same time as statutory sick pay so, if you have a company sick pay scheme, she will probably expect to receive payments under that scheme as well.

You have strong arguments for seeing through this particular MED3 – not least the fact that the employee admitted herself that her reason for not coming to work was that she didn't 'feel like' it.

You should ensure your contracts of employment allow you the discretion to withhold company sick pay in these circumstances. If your contracts do not allow you this discretion then withholding sick pay could well be viewed as a fundamental breach of contract entitling the employee to resign and claim constructive dismissal.

If your contracts of employment do not allow you the discretion to withhold company sick pay in these sorts of situations, you could still send a warning shot to the employee by sending her a letter telling her you are going to seek further information on her medical condition from her GP (see below) and warning her that, if you are not satisfied with the response, you might claim the sick pay back later.

Either way, you are entitled to write to the employee's GP challenging or at least questioning the diagnosis.

This is not to be confused with applying for a medical report from the employee's GP, for which you will require consent under the Medical Reports Act 1998. In this process you are asking for an explanation and elaboration of the sick note, and the doctor's qualification for making the diagnosis, but you are not asking for a medical report as such.

Although it may not make you popular with the GP, you are entitled to ask questions such as:

- What expertise do you have in diagnosing mental conditions such as stress?
- What examinations did you carry out in order to come to your diagnosis of 'stress'?
- Have you referred the patient to a consultant psychiatrist?

As above, you should really make sure your contracts of employment deal with these sorts of situations.

First, you should reserve the right to withhold company sick pay until you have had confirmation of any 'stress' diagnosis from a consultant psychiatrist. Second, you should make it clear that GPs' certificates will not be considered reasonable evidence to excuse an employee from attending any disciplinary or performance hearing, and that the only evidence you would accept is a report from a consultant psychiatrist confirming that the employee is too ill to take part in any such hearing or give instructions to anyone else to take part on their behalf.

See also page 149.

? Question

Your organization has just made Charles, the Regional Sales Manager, redundant. He has signed a compromise agreement which records the fact that he was redundant and he received a fairly generous ex gratia payment over and above his legal entitlements.

Three days after the compromise agreement was signed, your Sales Director has issued a press release welcoming a new Regional Sales Manager to the Organization, and Charles has read about this in the trade press. He writes you a furious letter pointing out that:

- His termination was clearly not a genuine redundancy.
- His replacement was obviously recruited before he had even left the organization.
- As a result of this misrepresentation the compromise agreement is null and void, and he is going to claim unfair dismissal at the Employment Tribunal.

Can he do this?

Solution █

There are two aspects of law that need to be considered. First, the law relating to compromise agreements, and second, general contract law. As far as compromise agreements are concerned, he cannot bring any claim as he has accepted the money in settlement of *any* unfair dismissal claims. It makes no difference that he now knows that success for his unfair dismissal claim would have been a certainty, rather than a likelihood. The uncovering of other facts after the signing of the agreement does not render it null and void.

A compromise agreement is, however, a contract. In extreme circumstances it may be possible for an employee to run an argument based on misrepresentation, under general contract law. In the 1999 case of *BCCI* v. *Ali and Others*, ex-employees of the BCCI sought to set aside compromise agreements waiving all claims for unfair dismissal, on the grounds that the bank had neglected to inform them of the fact that it was insolvent and carrying out a dishonest business at the time the Agreements were entered into. The employees' claims were based on the grounds of non disclosure, mistake and misrepresentation. The employees were, however, unsuccessful and the Court decided that there is no implied term under contract law requiring full disclosure by any employer. In the BCCI case the employees, like Charles, ran the argument that there was a misrepresentation on the basis that the position was not genuinely redundant. On the facts of the BCCI case the Court decided that the redundancies were genuine so, to that extent, Charles' point remains untested. Given the general flow of the decision in the BCCI case, however, it is highly unlikely that his claim to overturn the compromise agreement will be successful.

See also page 150.

Index